Alert and Attentive

Strategies to Support Focus and Concentration

Julie Tourigny, OTD, MS, OTR/L

www.gryphonhouse.com

Copyright

© 2025 Julie Tourigny
Published by Gryphon House, Inc.
P. O. Box 10, Lewisville, NC 27023
800.638.0928; 877.638.7576 [fax]
Visit us on the web at www.gryphonhouse.com.

All rights reserved. No part of this publication may be reproduced or transmitted in any form or by any means, electronic or technical, including photocopy, recording, or any information storage or retrieval system, without prior written permission of the publisher. Printed in the United States. Every effort has been made to locate copyright and permission information.

Cover and interior images used under license from Shutterstock.com.

Library of Congress Control Number: 2024952747

Bulk Purchase

Gryphon House books are available for special premiums and sales promotions as well as for fundraising use. Special editions or book excerpts can also be created to specifications. For details, call 800.638.0928.

Disclaimer

Gryphon House, Inc., cannot be held responsible for damage, mishap, or injury incurred during the use of or because of activities in this book. Appropriate and reasonable caution and adult supervision of children involved in activities and corresponding to the age and capability of each child involved are recommended at all times. Do not leave children unattended at any time. Observe safety and caution at all times.

Table of Contents

Introduction...**v**

Chapter 1: Attention: What It Is and Why It Matters..**1**

Chapter 2: Self-Regulation and Its Effects on Attention and Focus................**15**

Chapter 3: The Connection between Attention Span and Executive Function..**35**

Chapter 4: Environmental Considerations to Support Attention and Focus..**59**

Chapter 5: Sensory Inputs, Games, and Strategies to Support Attention and Focus..**75**

Chapter 6: Educational Games and Activities to Teach and Encourage Focus and Concentration...**95**

Chapter 7: Supporting Attention and Focus throughout the Day................**105**

References and Recommended Reading **120**

Index..**126**

Introduction

Hey! Hey, you! Yes, you! Over here! Pay attention!

As an early childhood educator, chances are you've used (or thought about using) one of these phrases as you try to gather the attention of the children you are working with. It can be challenging to get a class full of preschoolers to eat their meals and snacks in a timely manner. It takes a lot of work and planning to keep a class of three- to five-year-olds attentive for all of circle time. It's definitely difficult supporting a class full of kindergarteners as they complete learning activities within the time allotted. A primary reason for these challenges is because young children are still learning how to develop their attention skills.

Attention is the ability to focus on something specific while ignoring the nonimportant sights and sounds happening simultaneously. Good attention is necessary to learn and succeed at all of life's tasks. It helps us start and complete activities. It allows us to focus when we are engaged in a conversation in a noisy environment. Attention also keeps us safe from harm and injury.

When children struggle with attention, they may:

- Have difficulty completing work in a timely manner
- Find it hard to start activities on their own
- Miss key details when listening to instructions
- Have difficulty remembering rules and directions
- Exhibit disruptive and impulsive behaviors
- Distract children around them
- Appear forgetful or misplace things often
- Struggle to make and keep friends

As adults, we've become accustomed to blocking out the continual barrage of incoming sights, sounds, and sensations that are not relevant to what we are paying attention to. We ignore the feeling of our clothes and shoes, the swishing of our hair when we turn our heads. We ignore birds chirping outside, dogs barking, and conversations around us. Without thinking about it, we filter out the inputs that fill our field of vision so that we can remain alert and attentive to what matters to us.

Unlike adults, young children are learning to pay attention to what is important and to block out the irrelevant sights and sounds happening all around them. As they interact with the world, they are figuring out what they should ignore and what they should pay attention to. But, it is hard for them to not become distracted by competing sights, sounds, and feelings. Helping children learn how to pay attention supports their cognitive skills.

- When children are good at focusing, they are better able to absorb and retain information, follow instructions, and complete tasks to the best of their ability.
- Attention skills help children socialize, supporting their ability to listen carefully to others, respond to nonverbal cues, and participate in conversations.
- Learning how to focus and pay attention is important for self-regulation. Students can persist at activities that are challenging, control impulses, and maintain an alert and calm state of mind.
- Good focus is closely related to working memory, inhibitory control, and problem-solving, which are critical executive functions necessary for school success, social skills, and safety.

Consider the following: The majority of adults who have been driving for a long time are able to remain alert and attentive to what is going on around them so they can safely arrive at their destination. Most of the time, they are able to concentrate on the road and the other vehicles while listening to music or talking with people in the car. However, those same drivers may struggle to pay attention to the road during inclement weather. They may need to turn the music off or ask their companions to be quiet as they focus more intently on the road. This is also true for veteran drivers when they are traveling somewhere they've never been before. The need to focus on the road increases, and distractions become difficult to ignore, when we are driving somewhere new. The same is true for young children. When they engage in new tasks and activities (which is often), it is difficult to focus and attend to what they should while filtering out and ignoring the distractions around them.

People with good attention skills are not only able to focus on what they are supposed to, they are also able to concentrate on that for as long as they need to complete the conversation, activity, or task. This is not easy for young children, in part because they are learning this important skill and because they have a limited attention span. Therefore, it is easy for them to lose interest if an activity is too long, the environment is filled with an abundance of distractions, or the activity isn't one they want to engage in. Consider the following examples.

> Brayden transitions with his class to lunch. They eat in the cafeteria, which is just a short walk down the hallway from their kindergarten classroom. He sits down in his usual seat, observing everything going on all around him. The cafeteria is noisy, as many other classes are also eating at the same time. Children pop out of their seats, line up for hot lunch, and talk loudly with their classmates. After a few minutes, his aide notices that Brayden hasn't taken anything out of his lunch box yet, so she encourages him to start eating. Shortly after she walks away, someone at Brayden's table drops his milk carton and it spills all over the table. Instead of starting to eat, Brayden watches the commotion as people move away from the spill and the lunch monitor rushes over to clean it up. The lunch period ends and Brayden has eaten almost nothing. He gathers his lunch items and transitions out of the cafeteria with his class. Brayden exhibits difficulty with attention. Even though he doesn't disrupt or distract anyone, he has difficulty attending to what he should because he is paying attention to the sights and sounds happening all around him.

> One morning during circle time, Ayla sits on the carpet and plays with the toy she has taken from the pretend-play bin. She shows it to the children sitting near, shaking and spinning it around. When her teacher asks her to put the toy

where it belongs, Ayla complies. She returns to the carpet, sitting down in a new spot, and begins to talk with the child sitting next to her. The teacher tries to shift Ayla's attention to focus on circle time, but Ayla continues to play and talk, distracting the whole class. Ayla exhibits poor attention that affects her ability to attend to her teacher talking and concentrate on the circle-time activities.

Alivia has come to preschool sad. She had difficulty transitioning from her mother at drop-off and struggles to join her class to participate in the morning activities. During morning centers, Alivia sits at the table and asks repeatedly, "When is Mommy coming back?" Her teacher has put out an open-ended play activity using sand, shaving cream, and plastic farm animals that the whole class can engage in as they choose. Instead of interacting with the activity, Alivia continues to seek her teacher and inquire about when her mother will return. Alivia's attention is directed at when she will see her mom again, impairing her ability to concentrate on the activity in front of her.

How This Book Is Organized

Chapter 1 introduces the different components of attention—attention span, sustained attention, selective attention, and divided attention—and how each one is essential for children's success in learning, socializing, and completing daily activities. The chapter emphasizes that attention is not innate but improves with age and practice, making early childhood classrooms an ideal place for nurturing this skill. The remaining chapters explore strategies and tips to nurture and support the development of strong attention skills in young children.

Chapter 2 discusses the impact self-regulation has on attention. Self-regulation, the ability to remain calm and in control of thoughts, actions, and emotions in response to an external event or stimulus, is closely linked to attention and focus. When children are well-regulated, they are better at remaining alert and attentive to what they should be.

In chapter 3, we look at the connection between attention and executive function. Executive function is a group of mental skills that includes attentional flexibility, working memory, and inhibitory control. Children rely on these three executive functions to learn, play, and socialize throughout the school day as they:

- transition,
- take turns,
- practice self-control,
- problem solve,
- remain on task and complete activities in a timely manner,
- socialize successfully with peers and familiar adults, and
- negotiate conflict.

In chapter 4, you'll learn how the classroom environment impacts attention. You will learn ways to support children's ability to pay attention to what they should be with intentional classroom design, limiting visual and auditory distractions, and encouraging predictable classroom rules and routines.

Chapter 5 provides sensory-focused tips, ideas, and strategies that will help children attain and maintain an alert and attentive arousal level throughout their day.

Chapter 6 offers cognitive-behavioral strategies, games, and activities to support children's focus and concentration.

Finally, in chapter 7, you will learn simple and effective games, activities, and strategies to improve and support attention during specific parts of the school day, including mealtimes, circle time, and center time.

Use *Alert and Attentive* as a reference for strategies to help young children attend to what they should be so that they learn, play, and grow to the best of their ability. Rich with games, activities and easy-to-implement ideas, this book provides suggestions for environmental supports, sensory inputs, and cognitive behavioral strategies to help improve the attention skills of young children. *Alert and Attentive* also describes the relationship between self-regulation, executive function, and attention and the impact these have on one another.

Let's get started!

Chapter 1
Attention:
What It Is and Why It Matters

What exactly is attention? It is a person's ability to focus intentionally on something while tuning out the other sights and sounds happening at the same time. People rely on attention in almost all aspects of life: to pay attention at school, to complete work obligations, to finish chores around the house, and to socialize. In the early learning environment, children continually rely on attention. They use it when they focus on schoolwork or activities while blocking out classroom distractions. They use attention when socializing with peers because they need to focus on what's being said while tuning out nearby conversations. They also use it when listening to their teacher give important instructions or tell a story, while tuning out the other sounds around them.

Attention is not a skill that is present at birth. Rather, it improves and develops over time, with marked improvement between three and five years of age (Gomes et al., 2000; Krauzlis, Wang, Yu, and Katz, 2023; Posner, Rothbart, Sheese, and Voelker, 2014). This means the early childhood classroom is an excellent environment to help nurture and develop this critical skill. Over time and with practice, children learn how to recognize the difference between what is important to attend to and what should be ignored.

Consider the attention skills required of children as they play together during free time. During this time, children must focus on a play activity they chose while blocking out what other children in the classroom are doing. At the same time, they socialize with the children playing alongside them, focusing their attention to what is being said to them so they can make proper verbal responses. When the classroom teacher gives a five-minute warning alerting the class that free-play time will end soon, they must divide their attention on what she is saying and also continue to play as they have been without losing focus. When free time ends, children must stop focusing on what they have been, transition to the next activity, and become ready to focus and attend once again.

In this chapter, we explore the different components of attention, highlighting their crucial roles in children's ability to learn, interact socially, and handle everyday tasks. You'll also see how this skill is best developed over time through practice.

Understanding the Components of Attention

Attention is made up of multiple components that work together to help children as they focus on the correct task, person, or activity, sustain this concentration, and remain capable of shifting their attention to something different as needed. The components of attention include:

- attention span,
- sustained attention,
- selective attention, and
- divided attention.

Attention Span

Attention span refers to the amount of time a person is able to concentrate. In the classroom, it is the period of time children can concentrate before becoming distracted. As children age, their attention span increases (McClelland et al., 2013; Posner, Rothbart, Sheese, and Voelker, 2014). Not only does attention span improve as children age, but their ability to maintain focus on what is happening in the moment is a skill that children learn and become better at as they mature and practice. Children's attention spans may also vary depending on the activity and whether the child is hungry, tired, or bored.

Consider a time you've attended or listened to a training where the content didn't really apply to you. You may have struggled to pay attention. In contrast, if you've attended a training that was highly meaningful to your everyday life, you may have found it easy to focus and have a long attention span. The same is true for young children: When a task or activity is of interest or meaningful to them, children will demonstrate a longer attention span than when they are supposed to pay attention to something they are not interested in. The good news is, as children grow and practice, their attention span grows with them.

The average attention span by age is as follows:

- Two-year-olds: four to six minutes
- Three-year-olds: six to eight minutes
- Four-year-olds: eight to twelve minutes
- Five- to six-year-olds: twelve to eighteen minutes
- Seven- to eight-year-olds: sixteen to twenty-four minutes
- Ten-year-olds: twenty to thirty minutes

From two to four years of age, children's attention span has doubled. By the time a child reaches kindergarten, they should be able to focus on one activity for three times as long as they could when they were toddlers. In other words, the younger the child, the harder it is to attend to a task, activity, or conversation for long periods of time. With this in mind, children, especially very young children, should not be expected to pay attention to something longer than what is listed above. In the classroom, lessons and activities should extend for only as long as the average age of the children in the classroom. For example, in a multi-age preschool classroom of three- and four-year-olds, learning activities should last for up to eight minutes. Activities in a class of two- and three-year olds should last for a maximum of six minutes.

When children are not able to pay attention for an age-appropriate amount of time, they may:

- become distracted easily,
- abandon their work and activities before completing them,
- struggle to follow directions,
- have difficulty occupying their free time, and
- fail to develop strong play skills.

Sustained Attention

Sustained attention is a person's ability to concentrate on what they should do for as long as they need to without becoming distracted. For young children, sustained attention is the amount of time they can maintain their focus before they lose interest or become distracted. This is an important skill because it allows children to persist at attending to a task or activity even when it isn't highly interesting to them.

To understand sustained attention, let's think about how we use it while driving a car. Sustained attention helps us maintain our attention for the entire drive so we make it to the correct destination, whether it is five minutes or five hours away. We continue to focus on operating the car as we remain mindful of what is going on around us to stay safe, but not becoming distracted.

Sustained attention improves as children grow and have practiced focusing on one thing for a period of time. Two-year-olds are able to sustain their attention for four to six minutes. By six years of age, children can be expected to focus on one activity without becoming distracted for up to eighteen minutes (Posner, Rothbart, Sheese, and Voelker, 2014; Wray et al., 2017).

Sustained attention in can be impacted by boredom or visual and auditory distractions. A classroom is filled with visual and auditory distractions—children are talking while the teacher is talking, people walk by the classroom, an overhead fan whirls and clicks, toys are left out, and so on. These distractions are difficult for young children to ignore and can impact their ability to pay attention to what they should be for an age-appropriate amount of time.

When children struggle to sustain their attention for an age-appropriate amount of time, they may have difficulty with:

- staying on task,
- developing play skills,
- listening and following directions, and
- completing activities.

Selective Attention

Selective attention is a person's ability to focus on a particular object, item, or person while tuning out the other unimportant sights and sounds happening all around them. This type of attention helps people focus on what they should instead of the distractions that are occurring at the same time. Like the other components of attention, selective attention is a skill that improves over time and with practice. Young children are not good at selective attention because they are learning what is important to pay attention to and how to ignore distractions. They learn this skill as they interact with toys, peers, and adults while competing distractions exist at the same time. In the early learning environment, these distractions may be a toy, a favorite person, or other sights and sounds happening all around us all the time.

Let's get back in the car and see how selective attention helps us arrive at our destination on time and in one piece. While driving, we use selective attention to visually scan the road for the correct landmarks, street signs, or exit signs. We block out the signs and landmarks that are not relevant to us and pay attention to a sign that is important in helping us get to our destination.

Consider the following examples of children using selective attention in Ms. Murphy's and Ms. Claus's classes.

Ms. Murphy's preschool class has fifteen children. Most of the children turned three over the summer. Transitioning this group of young preschoolers from free play to circle time is always a challenge for Ms. Murphy. It takes a long time for the children to clean up, remembering to put toys where they belong. At least two or three of the children often refuse to put away their favorite toy. On average, it takes Ms. Murphy and her class ten minutes to end free play, clean up, and transition to the carpet. Ms. Murphy knows this is developmentally appropriate and recognizes that it is important to help her students learn how to clean up and how to transition from one activity to the next.

By four and five years of age, children are much better at ignoring distractions and intentionally attend to what they should be because they have been practicing selective attention for a few years now. By the second half of the school year, Ms. Claus's prekindergarten class has learned the classroom routine as they have followed the same structure all year long. When free time is close to ending, the children in this classroom are able to hear Ms. Claus's bell that she rings as a five-minute warning. Some of them begin to pick up, others continue to engage in their chosen play activity, trying to finish what they've started within the remining time left. When she cues them again, signaling that free time has ended, Ms. Claus's class is able to clean up as a group, putting toys where they belong with no resistance. Ms. Claus sits down at the carpet and bangs a gong indicating that circle time in beginning. The children transition over to the rug, sit down, and wait for circle time to begin.

The children in Ms. Claus's classroom have had time and years of practice following the rules and routines of the classroom. During this time, their selective attention has improved, which helps them finish playing during free time, clean up in a timely manner, and then transition to circle time independently.

As these examples highlight, selective attention supports goal-directed behavior. In the classroom setting, children rely on two main types of selective attention: visual selective attention and auditory selective attention.

Visual selective attention helps children visually focus on what they need to while ignoring nonrelevant objects close by. It helps children search for and find the right colored pencil. It is responsible for locating a specific toy in a crowded play space or a friend on a busy playground. For example, kindergarten students use visual selective attention while completing a letter search activity. If they are searching for and circling the letter *T* on a worksheet filled with a random selection of letters, children must focus on looking for that specific letter and ignoring or repressing the desire to circle letters that are not the letter *T*. To be successful with this activity, they must pay specific attention to the similarities and differences between the letters.

Auditory selective attention helps children home in on specific sounds, like a teacher reading a book, or a friend having a conversation with them, while blocking out the other noises happening in their earshot. This is an especially difficult skill for young children. It is difficult for two- to four-year-olds to filter out background noises and focus their attention on the teacher talking or reading or giving instructions. In a noisy classroom, or one that has frequent distractions, young children will find it difficult to focus on what they should and filter out these distractions.

When children struggle with selective attention, they have difficulty:

- developing strong play skills;
- making and keeping friends;
- occupying unstructured time independently;
- listening to, remembering, and following directions; and
- completing projects in a timely manner.

Selective attention can also be problematic when children focus on what they want to or what is right in front of them instead of what they should. Let's look at how a learning environment might impact children who are developing their selective attention skills.

Jeffrey is an only child who is young for his grade. For the past two years, he attended an in-home day care close to his house. Given these factors, Jeffrey is still working on developing his selective attention skills. This year, he has started kindergarten at the local elementary school. His kindergarten classroom is located on the first floor, right near the front office. The hallway outside his classroom door is busy with people traffic and noise. Jeffrey's teacher has designed the classroom in a way to try to minimize this distraction. Her desk is situated at the back of the class in a corner far from the front door. The whiteboard is placed on a wall adjacent to her desk so that when the children sit for circle time or large-group instruction, their backs are to the front door. This is sufficient for most children to pay attention while seated on the carpet. However, Jeffrey struggles to pay attention during circle time. He is almost always distracted by the activity happening in the hallway; often, instead of paying attention to what his classmates or teacher are saying, he is looking over his shoulder and out the door to focus on what's going on. Ms. Somerfield, Jeffrey's classroom teacher, has noticed that when the classroom door is closed, Jeffrey is an active participant at circle time. Similarly, when the hallway is quiet, Jeffrey is able to focus his attention on what is going on within the classroom.

Divided Attention

Divided attention refers to a person's ability to attend to more than one task or activity at the same time. Divided attention helps people engage in two or more activities that both require attention, such as preparing dinner while helping a child with homework or driving a car safely while listening to a friend talk about their day. Speaking of the car, let's explore how divided attention is used while driving. In the car, we rely on divided attention regularly. When there is a passenger in the car, we are able to carry on a conversation while driving safely to our destination. When we drive somewhere new, we are able to follow the directions to the destination while continuing to operate the car. When the music is on, we are able to listen and sing along to our favorite songs while driving safely.

In a class environment, children use divided attention to be successful with schoolwork and socializing with peers. In an early learning environment, few activities occur in isolation from anything else. Here are some examples of children using divided attention:

- Classroom teachers give new instructions while children are already engaged in an activity.
- Children listen and watch a movement video while copying the moves and steps.
- Students socialize with peers while eating their food during snack time.

Also referred to as *multitasking*, divided attention is one of the last components of attention to develop. It isn't until around age five that children are able to start multitasking successfully (Posner, Rothbart, Sheese, and Voelker, 2014; Wray et al., 2017). This means that before the age of five, it is difficult for children to focus and pay attention to two tasks or activities at the same time. The following example illustrates the difficulties many young children have when divided attention is required of them.

> Henry, a four-year-old preschooler, is a great eater. He eats a wide variety of foods and has a great appetite. At school, he and his class eat lunch together in the classroom as a group. During this time, he and his classmates are encouraged to socialize with friends; Henry seems to especially enjoy this time of the day. He laughs and talks with the children sitting with him at his table, sharing stories and ideas throughout the mealtime. However, his lunch tends to go uneaten. Many of the items in his lunch box are unopened, and within an hour of lunch ending, he is hungry.

Many young children, even kindergarteners, find it difficult to focus on both socializing and eating as their divided attention skills are still developing. In Henry's example, he is not able to focus on eating because he is attending to the social interactions happening all around him.

It is also normal for divided attention to be challenging when a task or activity is overly challenging. For example, a new driver may not be able to pay attention to operating the car while music is playing. Or a young child may not be able to carry on a conversation with a peer while playing outside on the playground. Other children may struggle to complete activities that require multiple steps such as coloring, gluing, and cutting, or paper tearing and gluing.

When children struggle with divided attention, they have a hard time attending to two or more important things at one time resulting in difficulty:

- listening to the teacher talking while they are working on a project,
- completing activities successfully and in a timely manner,
- answering questions correctly when called on,
- sticking with a task or activity, and
- completing activities made up of many steps.

> **Technology and Attention**
>
> Technology has a big effect on children's attention spans (Lodge and Harrison, 2019). Children who engage in a significant amount of screen time may become used to instant gratification, which can make it harder for them to focus on tasks that require sustained attention, such as reading a book or completing homework. Alerts and notifications from smart devices, such as phones, tablets, and watches, can easily pull children's attention away from what they should be doing. These distractions may lead to a lack of focus in class or while studying. Technology can take up time that might otherwise be spent on more focused activities, such as playing an instrument, reading, or engaging in imaginative play. Continual exposure to fast-paced content—rapid scene changes or action-packed games—can overstimulate the brain. This can make it harder for children to focus on less stimulating tasks, such as listening to a story or sitting quietly. Yet, when used mindfully, technology can enhance learning and creativity. It's all about balance (Lodge and Harrison, 2019).

Attention Skills Are Necessary All Day Long

Children rely on attention to be successful in every task or activity they engage in. They must inhibit attending to visual and auditory distractions while listening to the teacher give instructions for a seated activity. They must learn how to attend to their classwork while surrounded by classmates who might be coughing or sneezing, fidgeting in their seats, or walking around. Children must ignore what is going on in the hallway or outside the window to maintain focus on the task at hand, such as lunch or play. Furthermore, when children have a conversation with their peers, strong attention skills help them focus on what the peer is saying instead of all the other conversations and noises in the classroom.

This need for attention continues throughout the day. When children begin an activity, they must pay attention to that activity. Then, the activity ends. They stop paying attention to that task or activity as they transition to the next one. Then, they begin to pay attention again to this new task or activity. This happens all day long, day after day, year after year. While it is completely normal for attention to wander from time to time, children must learn how focus intentionally on what they should for an age-appropriate amount of time, switching their focus or multitasking when needed. They rely on sustained, selective, and divided attention to help achieve their goals, learn, play, socialize, and stay safe. Embedding games, activities, and strategies into early learning environments will help support this important skill so that children are able to remain alert and attentive to the best of their ability. In the following example, Mr. Tim successfully integrates different strategies to support his children's varying levels of attention skills.

> Mr. Tim teaches in a multi-age preschool classroom made up of three-, four-, and five-year-olds. During free time, James, a three-year-old, plays at the sensory table with dinosaurs and playdough while he listens to his classmate tell a story. He is able to divide his attention between the conversation and playing with his toy. When his friend says something really funny, James stops playing with the dinosaurs to laugh and listen to more of what his friend

has to say. James is able to play and listen for five or six minutes, then his attention diminishes. He moves away from the sensory table and wanders around the classroom for the remaining ten minutes of free time.

Parvati, however, a four-year-old in the same classroom, is able to spend time engrossed in building and constructing with two friends as they create a make-believe town. She invites her friends to join them, and they drive their wooden cars all around and through the town. When their teacher alerts the class that free-choice time is ending, Parvati cleans up and transitions with her classmates to the rug for circle time.

Mr. Tim is aware of this developmental difference as many of his older students are able to sustain their attention and focus for the duration of time each learning activity takes. He also recognizes that his younger students will not be able to sustain their attention or multitask well during free time. To help them remember to clean up their toys, Mr. Tim plays a "clean up" song. He gets down on the floor and helps the children clean up, modeling for them how to put the toys away in their proper place. Then, he encourages them to play follow the leader to help transition everyone over to the rug.

Attention, the ability to concentrate on something while blocking out distractions, improves as children learn and grow. Over time, children improve their ability to recognize the difference between what is important to focus on and what can be ignored. They learn to sustain their attention and block out distractions, and they are better able to divide their attention to focus on multiple things at once. Throughout their day, young children rely on attention to keep them safe and to help them succeed as they learn, play, and socialize with their peers. And, although it is normal for their attention to wander from time to time, children rely on attention throughout the day as they switch from play activities, mealtimes, rest times, and learning activities.

As attention is not a skill that is present a birth, but one that improves over time, early learning classrooms are places where children will struggle with attention at times. They are also excellent environments to teach and support the development of this critical skill. In the next chapter, we will take a closer look at the effect self-regulation on children's attention and ability to focus.

Chapter 2
Self-Regulation and Its Effects on Attention and Focus

Self-regulation is the ability to remain calm and in control of oneself when faced with big emotions. It is what allows children to remain in control of their emotions and responses when something happens that makes them feel embarrassed, angry, frustrated, or overly excited. This is an important skill because children who are able to regulate their emotions well are also better able to attend and focus on what they should after something happens that causes them to feel strongly. Having good self-regulation skills helps children calm down after an event or action that elicits a strong emotion so they are able to learn, play, and socialize to the best of their ability. Strong self-regulation skills help children with:

- improving attention and focus,
- managing behaviors and outbursts,
- making and keeping friends, and
- succeeding in school

Self-regulation helps children focus and maintain their attention span. It is a foundational skill that affects academic performance, social interactions, and participation. When children are well regulated, their attention and focus is better because they are able to:

- Resist distractions
- Persist at tasks
- Resist immediate gratification
- Control impulses
- Remain calm when they become frustrated or confused learning new or difficult material

Children with good self-regulation can better manage their impulses. Without self-regulation, they might give in to distractions more easily, which can interrupt their attention span. Well-regulated children are better at sticking with tasks, even when they are hard, boring, or frustrating. Instead of giving up or getting easily frustrated, they can push through challenges and continue focusing. Children with strong self-regulation are able to manage their emotional responses to stress or frustration. For example, if a child doesn't understand a concept in class, instead of becoming overwhelmed or giving up, a well-regulated child is able to stay calm, ask for help, and continue trying. This emotional control prevents feelings from getting in the way of attention, which helps children focus on solving problems or learning new information.

Furthermore, when children have strong self-regulation skills, they're better at motivating themselves and putting forth the effort needed to achieve a goal, even if it's difficult. This might look like a child who, despite feeling tired or bored, keeps working at learning how to read or form letters correctly because the child has learned to regulate their desire to quit or stop early.

Additionally, self-regulation also affects how well children focus and attend during group activities or social interactions. For instance, a child with good impulse control can listen to others, wait their turn in discussions, and follow social cues. Self-regulation allows them to stay engaged in the conversation or collaborative tasks without interrupting or getting distracted.

This chapter will explore strategies to nurture and support strong self-regulation skills as a way to improve focus and attention span throughout the school day.

How Self-Regulation Affects Children's Behaviors

Strong self-regulation skills support children's ability to focus and pay attention because when children are well-regulated, they are better able to pay attention and focus on what they need to rather than on the way they are feeling. Strong self-regulation also helps children sustain their attention on the task, activity, or conversation they are involved in for an age-appropriate amount of time. Finally, well-regulated children are better able to focus on what is relevant and tune out the distracting sights and sounds happening around them.

In contrast, children who struggle to regulate their emotions tend to have difficulty with sustained attention and focus because they are distracted by the intense emotions they are feeling. Children who are quick to become overly excited or upset during an activity tend to sabotage or abandon the activity at hand. When unable to remain calm and in control of their emotions and responses, children may have trouble attending to what they should for an age-appropriate amount of time. Consider the following example describing Marco, a bright and outgoing kindergartener who struggles with self-regulation.

> Marco is eager to learn and really likes socializing with his classmates. Most of the time, he is able to complete learning activities in a timely manner. He usually remembers the rules and routines the class has established, but these rules are different from the ones he has at home. He is an only child and his parents are divorced, so he splits his time between two separate homes. At school, Marco knows he must share, use kind words, and wait to be called on instead of blurting out an answer. But some days during morning meeting, he struggles with these rules because he is overly eager to share and doesn't want to wait to be called on. Other days,

Marco becomes upset with his classmates when he has to share limited resources during group activities.

One afternoon, during math centers, Marco grabs the counting bears from a classmate and demands that it's his turn. When the classmate asks for the bears back, Marco yells at the classmate. Hearing this, Ms. Johnson, the teacher, steps in to help. She asks both boys what is going on. Marco won't let the other child have a turn to speak. He yells, cries, and demands that it is his turn with the counting bears. Ms. Johnson speaks calmly to Marco as she reminds him to talk quietly and calmly and to give his classmate a turn to share his side of the story. Refusing to listen, Marco throws the bears at his classmate and runs away from the table.

Marco's difficulty regulating his emotions prohibits him from sustaining his attention on the math activity. Marco is unable to remain calm and focus on the math activity because he cannot wait for his turn to use the counting bears. Instead of making a well-regulated response, Marco is upset when Ms. Johnson tries to intervene, which leads to his disengagement from in the activity. His inability to regulate his emotions has caused him to miss out on learning during math time.

Young children will present with a wide range of self-regulation skills. Some will have strong self-regulation skills in almost all situations. Others, especially very young children, may become easily upset or overexcited throughout the day. Because early learning environments are unpredictable and young children are still learning how to control their emotions and reactions, there is a good chance every child will need help regulating their emotions at some point. Providing a nurturing and consistent environment rich in play and sensory activities that teach children to identify and respond to big feelings will support the growth and development of self-regulation skills.

The goal of teaching self-regulation skills is to help children learn how to remain calm and in control of their reactions no matter how mad, or sad, or overly excited they may become. The intention is not to teach children to avoid or repress strong feelings, because a well-regulated child, like a well-regulated adult, feels a wide range of emotions. Through nurturing interactions and intentional classroom instruction, children can learn how to manage their feelings, pay attention to what they should, and regulate their emotions and responses.

Children can learn to regulate their emotions through:

- modeling,
- identifying and understanding feelings,
- participating in open-ended play,
- using sensory inputs, and
- practicing coregulation.

Modeling

Modeling is a common strategy used in early learning classrooms to teach children new skills. Because most young children are visual learners, they learn through observation. Think about how one might teach a child to cut with scissors by modeling the action. First, the child might watch how to hold a pair of scissors correctly. Next, they observe how to snip by opening and closing the scissors with the fingers and thumb. Then, they watch how to hold a piece of paper in one hand and then cut or snip the paper using the scissors held in the other hand.

Similar to modeling how to use scissors correctly, when adults who are calm and in control of their emotions demonstrate to the children around them how they regulate their emotions, children have a model they can mimic. Further, when teachers define and describe their own emotions and model adaptive responses, students learn how to recognize and respond to their big feelings in similar ways. Modeling also helps children learn ways to react that are appropriate for the classroom environment. Modeling not only shows children that everyone has to manage strong feelings but also how to process and manage them on their own. Self-regulation may be modeled in the early learning environment throughout the day through demonstration and role-play.

Demonstration is a powerful tool to teach children how to manage big emotions, make a regulated response, control impulsive behaviors, and focus and pay attention to what is important in that moment. Showing children how you manage your feelings when something happens that makes you upset, embarrassed, or overly excited teaches them how they might react in a similar situation. It is also helpful for children to hear an adult narrate out loud how they are feeling, why they feel that way, and then model how to react, especially when something happens that elicits anger, sadness, embarrassment, or frustration. This helps children learn how to process and manage strong emotions when they experience them. Consider the following example showing how Ms. Hudson and Ms. Steph model self-regulation through demonstration.

> Ms. Hudson and Ms. Steph regularly model for their students how they manage their reactions when something makes them feel a big emotion. For example, one morning Ms. Steph has car trouble and arrives late to school. When she arrives, she lets the class know that she got a flat tire on the highway and had to wait for a service company to help her. She describes to the children how she felt, stating, "At first, I was scared because I heard a loud noise and didn't know what was happening. Luckily, I was able to pull over to the side of the road safely. After a while, I started to feel pretty frustrated because it was taking a long time for someone from the service company to come out and help me. I knew I was going to be late to work and felt upset about that."
>
> She pauses in her story to let the children in her class ask questions. Some of the children ask her what she did while she was waiting, so she explains how she managed her emotions and passed her time. Then, she continued with her story. "Once my tire was changed and I was able to start driving to school again, I felt relieved that everything was okay. I told myself that I was glad it was just a flat tire and nothing more serious."

Role-play is another method for modeling how to remain well-regulated while managing strong emotions. When children role-play, they take on the role or personality of another person. This might mean pretending to be a chef in a restaurant, or a cashier, or a teacher. In a classroom setting, children may naturally engage in role-play during free time. Teachers may also encourage role-play as a small- or large-group activity to teach self-regulation strategies. One way to accomplish this is through role reversal, where a child takes on the role of the teacher and the teacher assumes the role of a student in the class. Consider the following example of Mr. Cuevas (Mr. C to his students) using role-play to help his first graders persist at learning a new and difficult math concept.

> Mr. C has noticed that quite a few of his students are struggling to grasp how to subtract multiple numbers. Instead of persisting at the activity, some children are becoming so upset that they are abandoning their work and refusing to try. One morning at the start of math class, instead of beginning the lesson, Mr. C gathers the class together. He explains, "Today, we're going to practice what we do when we start feeling upset or frustrated. Let's pretend I am a student, and I'm going to show you what happens when my emotions get the best of me." Mr. C pretends to engage in a math problem he's put on the Smartboard. He acts confused, stomps his feet, crosses arms, and in a frustrated voice states, "Ugh! This math problem is too hard! I can't do it! I want to quit!" Mr. C then looks at the class, resumes his usual voice and demeanor, and asks, "What did you notice about how I was feeling and acting?"
>
> One student, Emily, raises her hand and says, "You looked really mad and didn't want to try anymore." Mr. C confirms that what Emily observed is correct. "That's right! When I get upset, it's important to stay calm and try to control my emotions so I can keep working." He then asks the class if someone could show him what he could do when he starts feeling frustrated in class. He pauses for a moment, giving the children time to think.
>
> Anoop suggests, "You could take a deep breath."
>
> Imani chimes in, "Or tell yourself it's okay that it's hard because it's new."

Katrina says, "Just tell yourself to just keep trying and you might get it right tomorrow."

Mr. C compliments each of the students who've offered solutions and then says, "Okay, I'm going to try this again. And, this time, I'm going to try to control my emotions so I don't get too frustrated and give up." Mr. C looks at the problem on the board again. He takes three deep, exaggerated breaths, and states, "Whoa! This math problem is really confusing." He takes a deep breath and continues, "But, I know I'm just learning how to do it." He takes three deep breaths again and says, "Plus, I know I can ask for help if I need to." He turns to the class and asks, "How did I do this time? What did I do to help myself calm down?" Many students raise their hands, and Mr. C calls on one to share their idea.

Serena says, "You took deep breaths and tried again. You didn't give up!" "Exactly!" exclaims Mr. C. "Taking deep breaths, asking for help, and not giving up are great ways to control our emotions when we feel frustrated. And remember, when you are learning something new, it's okay if it seems confusing and hard. For the rest of math class, I want to practice this together." He encourages the class to divide into small groups or find a partner. He instructs, "I want everyone to pretend you're having a tough time with something. Maybe it's a math problem like this one or a game you're playing. When you start feeling frustrated, try to take three deep breaths."

Mr. C's class spends the rest of the math period role-playing ways to combat frustration. While they didn't directly address the math lesson that day, Mr. C laid a strong foundation to help his students remain calm and in control of their emotions the next time they are working on something difficult.

Identifying and Understanding Feelings

In early learning environments, caregivers and educators teach young children important skills, including how to label and identify items such as colors, numbers, letters. Around this time, young children are also learning about their own personal likes, dislikes, and preferences. They do this through play, group projects, organized learning activities, listening to stories and books, and social interactions. These activities offer opportunities to teach children how to identify and understand feelings. Teaching children what feelings are, how to identify them, and that it is okay to feel strongly is an important step in understanding how remain calm and in control of big emotions. Once they understand this, children can learn to pause and think about what they are feeling, why they feel the way that they do, and then how they should react or respond.

To help children learn how to identify and understand their feelings, start by teaching children what feelings are. While children read or listen to books and engage in school activities, label and talk about feelings. Some children will already be able to identify a wide range of feelings, while this may be a new concept for others. Explore with children what makes people feel certain ways. While engaged in play, role-play, or when reading books, reflect on questions that explore in more depth what feelings are and why people feel them. The great thing about teaching young children about feelings is they are at an age where the enjoy reading books and listening to stories in which conflicts exist or characters make mistakes. These questions might include the following:

- What does happy look like? What does angry look like? What does afraid look like? What does excited look like? Encourage children to demonstrate with their faces and bodies what emotions look like to them.
- What makes people sad? Encourage children to explain events or situations that could make a person feel sad. Repeat for other emotions.
- What is (character in the book you're reading) feeling? How do you know?

This reflection might hard for some children, especially three- and four-year olds, to comprehend. Over time and with practice, the children will learn to identify and understand feelings within themselves and others around them. Next, help children learn to tune in to their feelings by helping them learn to identify how they feel when they feel it. Finally, teach ways to manage and react to big feelings. This can be done when reading books with characters with strong emotions and reactions, through storytelling, and role-play. Let's look at an example of storytelling Mr. LeRoy uses with his class.

> At circle time one day, Mr. LeRoy tells the class that, instead of reading a book, he's going to tell a story about two children he had in his class years ago. He describes the students, Danny and Colin, and tells the children that, although the boys were good friends most of the time, sometimes they had trouble getting along. Mr. LeRoy then asks the class if they want to hear about one of those times. Everyone eagerly agrees and Mr. LeRoy begins his story.
>
> Danny and Colin loved to play together. They played on the playground. They played together at the sensory table. They sat together at snack and lunch time. But their favorite thing to do was play with the dinosaurs. The T. rex was their favorite toy, and luckily there were always two T. rexes so they could each play with one.
>
> One morning, the boys could only find one T. rex. Colin got to it first, ran to the play table, and started playing. Danny searched everywhere for the second T. rex, but it was nowhere to be found. Danny didn't want to play with one of the other dinosaurs, so he went over to the table and asked Colin if he could have a turn. Colin said no and turned his back to Danny. Danny didn't like this. So, he ripped the T. rex from Colin's hand and ran away from the table.
>
> Mr. LeRoy pauses here and asks the class what they think happened next. So far, Mr. LeRoy has described the scenario, but he hasn't talked about how Danny or Colin were feeling.

He allows some children to state what they think might happen next and then resumes his story.

Colin got very upset. He jumped up, yelled loudly at Danny, "Give it back!" He pushed Danny to the ground, and then grabbed the T. rex back.

Mr. LeRoy stops his story and begins to ask the class questions.

- How were Danny and Colin feeling? How do you know?
- What happened to make these two good friends so mad at one another?
- What made Colin mad? Was it okay for him to feel this way?
- Why did Danny get upset? Was it okay for him to feel this way?

Mr. LeRoy spends time exploring with his class what Danny and Colin were feeling and why they felt the way they did.

Once students can identify feelings, they are ready to think about and understand why people, including themselves, feel the way they do. With this understanding, children can learn to pause and think about how they should respond rather than how they want to. These adaptive responses might be based on established classroom rules and social norms that they have been taught at home or in the classroom. This helps children learn that it is okay to feel strongly, but reacting strongly can be harmful to themselves and others. Teaching children this pathway to identifying and understanding feelings will help them develop self-awareness so they can pause before they react, giving them time to think about how they can react in a calm and well-regulated way.

For the rest of the week, Mr. LeRoy continues to talk with his class about Danny and Colin, asking questions to explore why they think the boys felt the way they did and whether their reactions were the right ones.

He asks open-ended questions, including:

- What did Danny do when he couldn't find another T. rex to play with?
- Was it okay?
- What could Danny have done instead?

Once children understand how to identify and understand feelings, they may be ready to learn how to replace big reactions with adaptive ones by teaching children to process their feelings.

- What am I feeling right now?
- What made me feel this way?
- What do I want to do?
- Is it appropriate?
- What have I learned how to do instead?

Participating in Open-Ended Play

Play experiences foster creativity, improve fine- and gross-motor skills, and enhance social skills in young children. Play, especially open-ended play, also cultivates self-regulation skills. *Open-ended play* refers to activities that have no set end point or specific purpose. When children engage in open-ended play, they succeed simply by being involved. These child-led learning experiences help children improve their ability to remain calm and in control of their feelings and actions. During open-ended play, children use their imaginations as they explore and interact with peers, toys, and activities without the threat of failure. In time, open-ended play helps children develop a toolbox of self-regulatory strategies that they can draw from when they need to. Open-ended play includes materials such as the following:

- Building with magnetic tiles, blocks, recycled materials, or nature items
- Dramatic play with a variety of props and costumes

- Animal figurines
- Playdough and modeling clay
- Sand and water table
- Shaving cream
- Fingerpaint and other art materials

In contrast, closed-ended activities have a specific product, timeframe, and rules to follow. These might include the following:

- Puzzles
- Books
- Art and craft kits that follow a step-by-step pattern
- Art projects with a model to follow

Providing children with opportunities to engage in open-ended play activities allows them to experience success simply by being involved in the activity. When children are able to interact and explore materials without the threat of failure, they are able to improve their skills because they are better able to focus on the play act instead of worrying about messing up or making a mistake. When children engage in open-ended play, they attend to the activity longer, explore materials more thoroughly, and connect with their peers authentically. At the same time, they learn how to take turns, to share limited resources, to improve communication skills, and what to do when they encounter something they dislike. Let's look at an example of this.

> Sadie, a five-year-old in Ms. Bradford's kindergarten class, struggles with fine-motor skills. She uses an atypical grasp when holding crayons, pencils, and markers. She struggles to open her snacks and always needs help getting the straw into her drink boxes. Sadie tends to avoid arts and crafts and abandons group activities that involve writing and drawing. Ms. Bradford spends a great deal of time encouraging Sadie to participate in these activities. When she abandons the activity by leaving the table, Ms. Bradford helps her transition back to her seat. Once there, Sadie

tends to refuse to engage in the activity and instead tries to socialize with her classmates. Ms. Bradford recognizes that Sadie is struggling to regulate her emotions when she becomes frustrated with activities involving fine-motor skills. She knows that Sadie needs practice to improve these skills, so she decides to use opportunities for open-ended play.

The class is learning about rainforests, so Ms. Bradford transforms the sensory table into a mini rainforest. First, she fills the sensory table with sand, stones, and some water. Then, she adds fake flower petals, leaves, and sticks. Next, she places plastic animals and bugs in the bin. She buries some of these in the sand, hoping Sadie and her classmates will search for them. Finally, Ms. Bradford places plastic tongs, spoons, scoops, tweezers, and paintbrushes in the table.

During morning meeting, Ms. Bradford introduces the class to the new activity. She demonstrates how they could use the tongs to grab a bug from the rainforest floor. She shows them how they might use the paintbrushes to brush away the sand and reveal a hidden rainforest animal. She lets them know that she wants them to have fun exploring their new mini rainforest. When it's Sadie's turn to play at the table, she engages with the materials in the sensory bin alongside her classmates, socializing and participating in the activity without becoming frustrated or upset.

Using Sensory Input

Enhancing the learning environment with multisensory inputs—meaning using multiple senses such as sight, sound, touch, and even movement—supports attention and focus in children in several important ways (Brandes-Aitken et al., 2019; Kaplan and Berman, 2010; McClelland et al., 2007). When children learn using multiple senses, they are less likely to become bored or distracted. This is especially important for young children, who are still working on improving their sustained attention skills. Integrating different sensory experiences—like allowing children to interact with manipulatives, move their bodies, or explore compelling visuals—keeps the brain actively involved in the learning process, which helps maintain focus. A multisensory approach helps children stay more focused and engaged in what they are learning, as their brain is processing the information in multiple ways, rather than relying on just one sense. Children are also more likely to remember information when it is presented through different sensory channels. For instance, if they hear a story while looking at corresponding images or physically manipulating objects related to the story, they're more likely to retain the information. Additionally, a multisensory learning experience also supports all types of learning styles, as not all children learn in the same way. Some are visual learners, while others are auditory or kinesthetic. By incorporating multisensory inputs into the environment, teachers can reach all types of learners more effectively. This inclusivity helps children feel more confident and engaged, which improves overall attention and focus, as they're learning in a way that suits them best.

There are four types of sensory inputs that can be incorporated into the day to support young children's self-regulation skills.

- Tactile or messy input
- Visual input and supports
- Auditory input and supports
- Movement

Tactile or Messy Input

Tactile, or touch, input is an excellent sensory input to add to learning activities as a tool to help children focus and maintain their attention on what they should. Adding a tactile component to seated learning activities will help children stay with the activity for the full amount of time and potentially engage more deeply. For example, when counting or engaging in a math activity, have children count and interact with physical objects, such as plastic bears, coins, or pompoms. During circle time, allow children to choose and hold a fidget toy to help them remain seated and attentive to the lesson being taught.

You also can use tactile input to help children calm down when their emotions get the best of them. When children are upset, sad, or embarrassed, engaging with tactile input can be a helpful way to provide a calming sensory break. Allowing children to engage with a tactile bin filled with sand or another dry, dense material will give them something soothing and purposeful to do until they can regain control of their emotions.

Visual Input and Supports

Visual sensory input is beneficial to help children who are feeling overwhelmed or dysregulated. Toys such as sand timers, glitter jars, liquid motion toys, and sensory tubes provide repetitive, soothing input that can help children calm down when they are feeling upset.

Visual input can also act as a support to help children with time management. Develop and maintain a consistent class schedule. Talk about the schedule regularly, and make sure to post the schedule in an easy-to-locate spot so children can reference it when they want to remind themselves what is coming up in the day. For children who are preliterate, include pictures along with words on the schedule. When children are able to manage their time, they are better at remaining calm and in control of their emotions, are less distracted, and are able to sustain their attention on what they should for as long as they are supposed to.

Limiting visual distractions in the classroom is another way to support attention, focus, and self-regulation for a group of very young children or those who are easily distracted. A clutter-free classroom automatically supports attention and focus because it removes unnecessary visual distractions. A classroom that has few decorations on the walls, has furniture placed in a way to allow for easy movement around the room, light from natural sources when possible, and toys and learning materials put away when not in use will support self-regulation skills and attention and focus.

Auditory Input and Supports

Auditory sensory input helps set the mood and tone of the classroom. A loud classroom with poor acoustics might make students feel overly excited and overstimulated, making it hard to attend to what they should be (Lin, 2022). Children in noisy classrooms tend to have more difficulty sustaining their attention and are more easily distracted (Shield and Dockrell, 2008). Research has shown that noise can significantly affect students' ability to concentrate, process information, and sustain their attention on the task at hand (Shield and Dockrell, 2008). Adding carpet, curtains, or foam panels to the classroom may help reduce the noise level of the classroom because these absorb sound and reduce noise happening both within and outside the classroom. Play white noise or quiet music while students are engaged in quiet, seated activities or during rest time. For students who are easily distracted by environmental noise, doing so may block out or muffle the distracting sounds such as children coughing or sniffling, chairs scraping, and teachers tidying up the space (Lin, 2022).

Another auditory strategy that can help children sustain their attention and focus is to model a calm and quiet voice when talking. Studies show that learning in a loud environment can be distracting for many children (Shield and Dockrell, 2008). It is normal for young children to speak loudly in a loud environment, so modeling a quiet voice may help them speak more quietly and listen more intently to what is being said to them and will quiet down the whole room when needed.

Set clear guidelines for when and where certain noise levels are acceptable. Consider using a consistent nonverbal cue, such as raising a hand or ringing a bell, to signal that it's time to be quiet. Another auditory strategy is to create areas in the classroom, such as group work areas, where noise is allowed and areas where silence is required, such as independent workstations. Consider adding visuals to support this understanding, for example, a traffic-light system in which a green light means talking is allowed, yellow means quiet voices, and red means silence.

Movement

Enhancing activities with opportunities to move their bodies helps children be better prepared to attend to, learn, and retain information. The more students move their bodies throughout the day, the better able they are at attending to a seated activity. Many kindergarten schedules allow for only twenty minutes per day of recess, which is too little time for most children to get all the movement input their bodies need to stay alert and calm during the entire school day. Adding movement opportunities to the regular school day and learning activities will support strong self-regulation skills.

Activities such as dancing, walking on a balance bar or tape on the floor, obstacle courses, and swinging improve gross-motor coordination, cooperation with peers, and listening skills. For those children who are fidgety and wigglers, consistently moving their bodies throughout the day helps them sit longer and focus on what they are learning. When the school day is filled with regular opportunities for children to exercise and move their bodies, they will be better prepared to learn and retain information.

Practicing Coregulation

Coregulation refers to the nurturing interactions young children have with familiar and trusted adults when they struggle to understand, express, or manage their thoughts, feelings, and behaviors on their own. When children cannot manage their emotions, coregulation can be an effective strategy to help them calm down. The purpose of coregulating is to be together in a difficult moment so that the caregiver can lend their calm state to the child to help them work through feeling very upset, mad, frustrated, or overly excited. Simply sharing space in the moment and lending the dysregulated child your calm state of mind will help them. This way, you are showing, not telling, the child how to calm down.

To be effective, the caregiver should remain calm and in control of their own emotions when attempting to coregulate with a child cannot calm down on their own. Talk quietly and slowly with the child, modeling for them deep breathing and a calm state of mind. To further support children through coregulation, consider engaging in a repetitive, calm activity with the child, such as:

- Going for a walk
- Taking slow, deep breaths
- Tossing a bean bag back and forth
- Bouncing on an exercise ball while seated
- Completing a series of wall push-ups together

Consider this example describing Ms. Steph and Ms. Hudson's classroom. Both teachers use coregulation to help the children in their classroom calm down when they struggle to do so on their own. This helps the individual children and the class as a whole focus and pay attention to what they should be instead of the big feelings they might be experiencing.

> Ms. Hudson's prekindergarten classroom is full of children with big emotions. One of the students, Kayla, often enters the classroom sad, not ready to separate from her grandmother, who always drops her off in the morning. She needs help placing her things in her cubby and finding something to do to occupy her time as she waits for the rest of her classmates to arrive. By late morning, another child, Harper, tends to get wiggly and has trouble paying attention during circle time. She often interrupts Ms. Hudson to express how excited she is for snack and outdoor time. Harper tends to focus on these upcoming activities instead of participating in the current activity. Max loves building and constructing during free-play time. But he is easily frustrated when his block tower falls over or the road he's created doesn't stay in place.
>
> Ms. Hudson and her teacher's aide, Ms. Steph, use coregulation to help each of these children find ways to manage their big emotions. Most mornings, Ms. Steph asks Kayla to walk around the classroom with her to water plants or pick up toys. She knows that Kayla is too upset to occupy her time

well on her own, so she spends time with her, breathing deeply and talking quietly. Before circle time starts, Ms. Steph leads a small group of children, including Harper, in a movement activity. She models how to do wall push-ups and encourages them to copy her. During free-choice time, Ms. Hudson intentionally spends time building alongside Max. When his tower falls down and he becomes upset, Ms. Hudson acknowledges that the tower fell by nodding her head. She closes her eyes, breathes deeply for a breath or two and then asks Max if he'd like her to help him rebuild what he was making. These simple acts of coregulation not only help Kayla, Max, and Harper control their big emotions, they also help every student in the classroom recognize the importance of a calm and in-control response.

Self-regulation is responsible for helping children control their reactions when faced with a big emotion. Strong self-regulation skills support children's attention through the ability to stay on task and focus on what is relevant while ignore distractions and impulses. Teaching young children self-regulation skills can be done through modeling and coregulation, as well as teaching children how to recognize and identify feelings. Creating a learning environment rich in open-ended play and sensory inputs will support the development of strong self-regulation skills so that children learn ways to manage their emotions no matter how frustrated, mad, or overly excited they become.

In the next chapter, we will explore how executive functions affect attention and focus, defining what executive function is and discussing how to support its development in early learning environments. You will also learn strategies to promote strong executive functioning throughout the day, ensuring children remain alert and attentive to their activities.

Chapter 3
The Connection between Attention Span and Executive Function

Executive function is a set of mental skills that help people manage and regulate their thoughts, emotions, and actions. Executive function helps people pay attention, plan ahead, organize tasks, control impulses, and adapt to changing situations. Good executive function skills also help people remember what they need to, attend to what they are supposed to, and maintain control over their thoughts and actions so they can be successful in planning, completing, and executing goal-driven activities. Children rely on executive function skills to learn, play, and socialize throughout the school day. Children with strong executive function skills are better at problem-solving, socializing, and completing schoolwork successfully.

This chapter describes why executive function is essential for helping children with focus and attention. We will look at these three executive function skills and the role each plays in supporting attention skills.

- **Attentional flexibility** refers to the ability to shift focus between tasks and adjust to changing demands, helping them stay on track even when distractions arise.
- **Working memory** is the ability to hold on and manipulate information, like remembering instructions or keeping a goal in mind while performing tasks. This skill is crucial for maintaining attention to a task over time.

- **Inhibitory control** is the ability to resist impulsive reactions and regulate emotional responses. This skill helps children remain calm and focused rather than acting out or getting distracted.

Although each of these skills plays a distinct role, they collectively contribute to children's goal-directed behavior, their ability to self-regulate, pay attention, and focus.

Attentional Flexibility

Attentional flexibility is the ability to switch focus from one person, task, or activity to another in response to a change in situation. Children with age-appropriate attentional flexibility are better at paying attention to what they are supposed to, filtering out distractions, reacting well to disruptions to the normal routine, playing in new ways, and problem-solving. They are also able to be flexible when something, such as a fire alarm, a spilled drink, or an abrupt change to the routine, requires them to shift their attention to something else. Attentional flexibility is comprised of three skills:

- Flexible thinking
- Filtering
- Task switching

Flexible Thinking

Flexible thinking is a skill that helps children with problem-solving, learning new things, and shifting gears when what is supposed to happen doesn't. Children who have no trouble adjusting to change are flexible thinkers. They easily adapt to different situations, such as adjustments to the school schedule or sudden changes in plans. This is an important skill because even with a predictable classroom routine, the school day can change, and children encounter situations that require flexible thinking. In contrast, children who struggle with flexible thinking tend to be rigid in their thoughts and actions, which can lead to frustration when unexpected events occur. This rigidity can negatively impact children's ability to concentrate and focus.

Filtering

Filtering is responsible for distinguishing between important information and distractions. In a classroom setting, distractions typically come from visual and auditory inputs occurring throughout the day. They include things like people passing by in the hallway, conversations the child isn't part of, activities going on outside that the child might observe through a window, fans spinning, or heaters clicking on and off.

Children who struggle with filtering may have difficulty concentrating in a noisy and/or visually distracting classroom because, instead of paying attention to what they should, they expend mental energy focusing on everything at once: the visual distractions, sounds and conversations occurring throughout the classroom, *and* the activity they should be working on.

Task Switching

Task switching is the ability to shift attention from one activity to another. This skill helps children transition from activity to activity with ease. For some children, switching focus from one task to the next is simple. These children are able to redirect their attention as needed to engage in activities for as long as they should, then transition away from that activity, and refocus on the next task or activity. However, task switching is a challenging skill for many young children because they have not had enough experience transitioning away from preferred activities to do so with ease. For many young children, switching to a new activity, cleaning up when it is time to, and transitioning to a non-desired activity can be difficult and frustrating and may lead to decreased engagement in the new activity.

Working Memory

Working memory, a type of short-term memory, refers to the small amount of important information children need to retain to successfully engage in cognitive tasks and classroom activities. Working memory is like a mental to-do list, with the information stored only as long as it is useful. Once it is no longer needed, the to-do list disappears, freeing up space so that the child has the capacity to take in new and important information. Children who have strong working-memory skills are better at recalling and following directions, organization, problem-solving, and sustaining their attention to complete tasks and activities. When children have strong working memory skills, they are also better at dividing their attention between multiple tasks and activities. For example, they can eat their lunch while holding a conversation with a classmate.

When children have challenges with working memory, they may struggle to keep track of what they are supposed to do. Children with poor working-memory skills may also find it difficult to stick with and complete tasks on their own.

Supporting Working-Memory Capacity

Working memory determines the amount of items the brain can store and remember at one time. It varies among individuals, influencing how much information they can hold and manipulate at once. Working memory is crucial for learning, problem-solving, and decision-making. Young children are only able to hold a limited amount of information in their working memory at any given time. It's important to recognize the limitations of children's working memory based on age and experience and to avoid requiring them to remember too many rules or difficult routines. In addition, when an activity is novel, each step needs to hold a place in a child's working memory. Children who have experience with an activity may remember some or all of the steps necessary to complete it, a skill known as *chunking*. Rather than needing to remember every step of the activity, children with prior knowledge can chunk together all or part of it.

Techniques that support young children's working-memory skills include:

- Breaking tasks and activities into smaller steps
- Using visual aids that depict the items required to complete a project
- Explaining the steps required to complete an activity and then asking children to repeat them back before starting the activity

Inhibitory Control

Inhibitory control refers to a person's ability to stop and think before reacting. In the classroom, inhibitory control helps children control their actions and behaviors so they are able to respond in a way that matches the task, activity, or social situation. Inhibitory control is also responsible for children's ability to focus on what is relevant, such as a teacher's explanation of a group activity, while ignoring ongoing visual and auditory distractions occurring at the same time. Children with strong inhibitory control can wait their turn, control their impulses, and persist at activities. They attend to what their teacher is saying or engage in a conversation with a friend while blocking out the unimportant visual and auditory events happening all around them.

When children struggle with inhibitory control, they may act impulsively and ignore the classroom rules and established routines to get what they want right when they want it. They may overreact when games and activities don't go their way, or they may throw tantrums. Their schoolwork may be rushed, and they may be easily distracted, focusing on everything going on around them instead of the task at hand.

Executive Function, Attention, and Focus

Attention, focus, and executive function are closely related. Executive function provides a framework necessary for children to effectively manage their attention skills, leading to improved focus, productivity, and academic performance. When children have strong executive function skills, they have the mental capacity for age-appropriate attention and focus. In contrast, when children struggle with executive functions, they may have difficulty with sustained attention, focusing on what they should, ignoring distractions, and multitasking.

Attentional flexibility helps children prioritize what is relevant and ignore the distractions happening all around them. It is also responsible for sustained attention by helping children remain on task or switch gears when appropriate when they grow bored or frustrated.

Working memory supports attention and focusing skills by helping children remember important information that is needed to complete activities and schoolwork. It also helps children engage in and have successful social interactions. Working memory also supports children's divided attention as the better a child's working memory is, the better they are at multitasking.

Inhibitory control helps children maintain attention and focus as they prioritize what they should be paying attention to rather than what they may want to. It supports sustained and selective attention and helps children complete the tasks and activities they should be.

Classroom Strategies to Support Executive Function

Executive function develops throughout childhood, so young children will need guidance and support to strengthen these skills. Activities that encourage children to follow instructions, take turns, and problem solve can help promote the development of executive function skills. Young children may struggle at times with sustained attention, impulse control, completing tasks on time, and staying organized. But with the right type of support and opportunities to practice, they are capable of improving their executive function abilities.

In an environment that supports executive function, children are better at flexible thinking, self-control, and remembering what they need to. They are also better at paying attention to what they are supposed to. Strategies and activities that nurture the development of executive function skills include the following:

- Metacognition
- Modeling
- Role-play
- Time management

Metacognition

Metacognition, the awareness of one's thought process, is an effective way to improve young children's attention, and focus. Teaching children how their senses help them focus and pay attention, using language that makes sense to them, will support the development of these skills. Commanding young children to sit still, or focus, or listen is not effective when they have not learned how to focus and pay attention. Instead, use metacognitive strategies to teach children how to learn what it takes to focus their attention on what they should. This includes teaching children what attention and focus are and how children use their brain, eyes, and ears to help them be good at focusing and paying attention. Then, when children understand why attention and focus are important and how they use their eyes, ears, and brain to help focus and pay attention, cue children before an activity starts that they will need to use their ears to listen, their eyes to see, and their brain to remember.

One way to improve young children's metacognition is to encourage them to "turn on" their senses. Teaching children to think about what senses they need to be successful in listening, seeing, focusing, and remembering will improve their attention skills. Before teaching a new activity, talk with children about how they might think about and focus on the things they need to be successful. Teaching children to think about paying attention and remembering, and then cueing them to actively think about the skills they need before starting an activity, is a useful metacognition strategy that helps children improve their focus and attention skills. The following activity can be used as a tool to help children visualize the senses they use to remember and focus.

Techniques for teaching children the metacognition skills they'll need to support strong executive functions include encouraging self-reflection through intentional self-talk and cueing. Cueing children before an activity starts that they will need to use active listening, memory, and patience skills can help them become more self-aware and intentional in their learning and interactions.

Active listening is a key component of executive functioning because it helps children focus, understand, and process information more effectively. Cue children before an activity starts to help them mentally prepare to engage their attention fully and thoughtfully. Techniques to cue active listening include:

- Verbal reminders: Before a listening task, remind the children of the specific listening behaviors you expect. For example, "I want everyone to practice really listening today. That means no interrupting. Think about what the other person is saying before you speak."
- Post visual cues: Post a simple chart with pictures or icons representing the components of active listening, such as "eyes on the speaker," "ears open," "hands still," as a visual reminder.
- Modeling: In addition to telling children, modeling is a strategy to show children what active listening looks like. For example, Ms. McKenzie wants her first-grade class to listen to one another when they share and ask questions during math class. Before the lesson starts one afternoon, she asks the class to watch her as the class assistant, Ms. Sarah, explains the lesson. Ms. McKenzie states, "Okay everyone, watch me as I listen closely to Ms. Sarah." She pauses and then looks intently at Ms. Sarah and then continues, "I want you to notice how I don't interrupt and how I ask a follow-up question based on what she said."

Working memory, another crucial executive function skill, helps children retain and apply information over time. Cueing children to use their working-memory skills may help them focus ozn the importance of storing and recalling key details, which is essential in both academic and social situations. Techniques to cue working-memory skills include verbal reminders. Before starting any task where memory will be needed, provide a cue such as, "In this activity, you're going to need to remember some important details. Take a moment to think about how you'll keep those facts in your mind." Encourage children to ask themselves, "What do I need to remember?" before starting a task and after completing it.

Controlling impulses and maintaining focus is another important executive function that metacognition can help improve. Cueing children to practice remaining patient when they are bored, activities are challenging, or when things take longer than expected can help them with sustained attention and focus. Techniques to cue inhibitory control include the following:

- Clear expectations: Before any task that requires patience, such as waiting for their turn or working through a difficult problem, provide a cue such as, "In this activity, you'll need to be patient. You might not get the answer right away, and that's okay. Take your time and stay calm as you work through it."
- Mindfulness cues: For moments where impatience might arise, such as when waiting for others to finish, offer strategies to help children cope. "If you feel impatient, try taking three deep breaths and reminding yourself that everyone needs a chance to finish."
- Praise patience: When children demonstrate patience, offer specific praise such as, "Zack, I noticed you waited quietly while others were speaking. That was a great way to practice patience!"

Another technique to support metacognition is to encourage children to talk themselves through tasks. This self-talk helps them monitor their own thinking and process how they are using these skills. Try self-talk prompts such as the following:

- "What should I be listening for right now?"
- "How can I remember what they just said?"
- "Am I staying patient? What can I do to wait my turn more calmly?"

Cueing and modeling for children before an activity begins is a powerful way to help them develop metacognition skills that support executive function skills. By setting clear expectations, providing visual or verbal cues, modeling the desired behaviors, and creating opportunities for practice and reflection, teachers can foster a classroom environment where children become more self-aware and in control of their thinking and actions.

Modeling

Modeling is an effective strategy that helps children learn how to remain flexible when things don't go their way, how to prepare for a new activity, to persist with difficult or boring tasks, or to be patient when they are eager to do or say something. By watching teachers model and describe their emotions and thought processes, children develop a framework they can draw from when they face similar situations. Sharing thought processes, reminding themselves to be flexible thinkers, actively listening, and waiting patiently are examples children can copy when they need to switch gears, try something new, or play a different way. Talking about changes and disruptions when they occur, and then demonstrating how to deal with them, is a valuable tool teachers can use so children learn how they can and should act.

Educators can model attentional flexibility by demonstrating adaptability and shifting focus as needed. You can demonstrate flexible thinking by being open to different ideas, trying new things, and adapting to changes. Children learn by example, so narrating your flexible mindset can influence theirs. Here are some ways you can use modeling to help your students learn attentional flexibility skills:

Model task switching. Think about and describe how you transition from one activity to another, even if you aren't finished or don't want to.

Model flexible thinking. When a change in the usual routine or something unexpected occurs, narrate your thoughts about the disruption. For example, let's say you forgot your lunch at home, something you put together the night before and were really looking forward to eating today. Describe out loud your thoughts and feelings: "Oh no! I just realized that I forgot my lunch at home. I feel really frustrated with myself right now because I really wanted to eat what I made." If the children are curious and ask, you might explain what you had packed and why you like that particular food so much. Then, describe how you will have to be flexible and eat something different. For example, you might say, "Even though I really wanted to eat the lunch I packed, I will have to eat something else so I have enough energy for the rest of the day. I think I will eat a hot lunch today and hopefully I will remember to bring my lunch tomorrow."

Modeling inhibitory control for young children helps them gain awareness and insight into their own abilities to control their impulses in different situations. The following are ways you can model impulse control during a typical school day:

Model rule following. Talk about how you follow the established class rules. Explain why rules are important for maintaining a positive and safe learning environment. As you follow rules throughout the day, state out loud what you are doing. For example, when the class lines up to transition out of the room, line up with them. Consider pointing out to the class that you are standing quietly in line with your hands to yourself. Remind the class that following the rules by standing quietly in line keeps you and others around you safe, attentive, and ready to go when it is time to.

Modeling is an effective strategy that shows children the behavior expected of them. Consider this example highlighting how Ms. Holly, a first-grade teacher, uses modeling to help her students control their impulses during large-group instructional times.

> Ms. Holly, a first-grade teacher at a small charter school, prefers teaching her class new material while they are seated together on the carpet rather than in their chairs. She adopted this approach years ago because she enjoys bringing her students together as a large group for learning. However, this year, a few of her students have had difficulty with impulse control. Instead of raising their hands to answer questions, they blurt out their replies. When they are confused, they talk over her while she is explaining the lesson. Ms. Holly has reminded the class of the importance of raising their hands and explained why it's necessary to wait to be called on. Still, some students continue to blurt out and talk over one another.
>
> One afternoon, as the class gathers on the rug for a math lesson, Ms. Holly announces that Ms. Courtney, the class

aide, will be joining the students to learn alongside them. Ms. Courtney sits on the rug with the students, modeling how to sit quietly with her eyes focused on Ms. Holly. Ms. Holly explains, "Ms. Courtney is going to show us how to raise our hands when she wants to speak because this helps everyone have a turn and listen to each other." She then reminds the class that they can raise their hands when they want to say something, ask a question, or answer a question. As Ms. Holly begins the math lesson, the class observes Ms. Courtney, who is sitting quietly with her visual attention on Ms. Holly. When Ms. Holly asks a question, Ms. Courtney slowly and calmly raises her hand. Ms. Holly calls on a few students who have raised their hands. Ms. Courtney has modeled remaining patient as keeps her hand raised and listens to the other children's responses. Finally, Ms. Holly calls on Ms. Courtney. She listens to her response and praises her for both raising her hand and waiting patiently to be called on. By modeling this behavior, Ms. Courtney demonstrates how to control the impulse to blurt out answers, helping the students understand both the physical action of raising their hands and the importance of waiting their turn in a respectful manner.

Role-Play

Role-play allows children to practice important social skills such as cooperation, sharing, taking turns, and empathy. Encourage pretend-play scenarios in which children have to remember their roles, the rules, and/or specific sequence of events. Encourage them to work together and solve problems collaboratively. Sometimes, children may need guidance during role-play to help them navigate social interactions or resolve conflicts. Start by demonstrating how to engage in role-play. Act out scenarios with a few students to show how they can pretend to be different characters and interact with each other. Step in as needed to provide gentle guidance and support.

Role-play challenging situations such as sharing a highly desired toy, participating in fire drills, or sticking with an activity when it is hard.

Pretend to be in situations in which a child needs to wait, take turns, or resist temptations, and model appropriate responses and behaviors.

To encourage working-memory skills, encourage role-play in which children use their imaginations and creativity. Encourage them to come up with their own scenarios and characters. To facilitate this in an early childhood classroom, consider dedicating a corner to role-playing scenarios. This might be set up as a kitchen, doctor's office, grocery store, or anything else that interests the children. Change the themes of the role-playing area regularly to keep it exciting and engaging for the children. Remember to stock the play area with props and costumes related to the theme. For example, in a kitchen area, include toy pots, pans, utensils, and play food. Costumes like chef hats and aprons can enhance the experience. For kindergarten and first-grade classrooms, consider introducing role-play activities during circle time or while seated on the carpet as a whole class.

Time Management

Time management is an excellent way to support strong executive function skills, even in the preschool classroom. Few if any young children will know how to tell time, but they can learn time-management skills, which will improve their sense of control over their day, help them participate better in all parts of the day, help them transition with ease, and support them to stay focused on what they should. When we give children tools to manage their time well, they are better at skills such as the following:

- Self-control
- Transition skills
- Patience
- Sustained attention to task

The following are strategies to help children manage their time throughout the day.

- **Establish a daily routine.** Creating and following a daily schedule helps children feel confident and in control of their school day. When children understand and are able to predict what will happen next, they feel more confident and in control of their day.
- **Develop and post visual schedules outlining the activities of the day.** Display visual schedules comprised of pictures so children can see the sequence of the activities of the activities they will participate in. Children feel a sense of confidence and security when they understand what their day entails and what to expect next. This helps with patience, focus, and transitions.
- **Consider using a transition cue to help children with smooth transitions.** Use transition cues, such as a bell or song, to signal for children when it is time to move from one activity to the next. Using these cues consistently will help children transition smoothly and independently.
- **Utilize timers throughout the day.** Use visual timers, sand timers, or stopwatches to help children understand the concept of time and manage their time during activities effectively. Incorporating timers into activities helps children visualize how long they have left to complete an activity and how much time they have to wait until the next activity starts. This helps with self-control, patience, and transitions.

Activities to Support Attentional Flexibility

To improve flexible-thinking skills, consider engaging children in games or activities that encourage them to think about doing something or using something in different ways. Use consistent language so it can be generalized to situations that may arise when children become inflexible or rigid in their thinking. Here are two activities that you can incorporate into your weekly lesson plans.

Activity: Can We Do It a Different Way?

The first few times children engage in this activity, they will benefit from hearing about how common games, jobs, or activities can be done in different ways. For example, there may be more than one way to walk to the lunchroom or auditorium or more than one way to water the classroom plants. You can do this activity with a few children in a small group, or do it with the whole group during circle time.

Intended Outcomes:

- Children will improve flexible thinking.
- Children will improve task-switching skills.
- Children will maintain attention and focus on what they should when things do not go their way.

Materials:

- None

What to Do:

1. Let the group know that you are going to challenge them to think up new and different ways to do the things they always do. Describe a scenario that highlights how the activity or job you are talking about is usually done. For example, you might ask to them to think about how to water the class plants. Discuss how they typically do this class job.
2. When they finish sharing, ask, "Now, what would you do if the watering can were missing? The plants still need to get watered, or they could die, so we have to think of something." Encourage them to be creative and visualize new ways to complete the task.
3. Encourage the children to share their ideas, prompting them with possibilities if they get stuck. In the plant-watering example, the children may suggest:

- Asking to borrow a watering can from the class next door
- Putting the plants in the sink and watering them from the faucet
- Watering the plants using a plastic cup

4. Praise each idea and suggestion using language that encourages and support flexible-thinking skills.
5. This activity can be approached in a variety of ways, including considering activities or times of the day that cause children to feel inflexible in their thinking. Common situations where young children may act rigid or inflexible in their thinking might include:

- Playing at recess in different ways
- Playing with new toys during free-choice time
- Sitting in a different spot during circle time
- Walking to familiar places throughout the school grounds in new ways

Once children are familiar with this activity, encourage them to apply this concept when they are faced with a challenge to their attentional flexibility. For example, if a disruption to the normal routine occurs because a guest speaker is scheduled to visit, ask, "We always have free time, then centers, then snack. If we have a guest speaker come in to talk with us this morning, how can we do our routine differently?"

Activity: What Else Can It Be?

Intended Outcomes:

- Children will learn that items can have more than one use.
- Children will improve flexible-thinking skills.
- Children will improve task-switching skills.

Materials:

Any item that could be used in a different way, such as:

- Paper towel (could be a blindfold, bandage, doll blanket)
- Plastic cup (could be a watering can, home for a small stuffie or toy animal, mountain for a toy animal or person to climb, parking garage for a toy car)
- Pencil (could be a magic wand, balance beam for a small toy animal or person to walk across)

What to Do:

1. Gather children in a small group or do the activity during circle time. Tell them that you are going to challenge them to think up new and different ways to use familiar objects.
2. Bring props so children can visualize how they typically complete the activity. Describe a scenario that highlights how the familiar object is usually used. For example, hold up a pencil and describe how it is used for writing and drawing.
3. Ask children how they usually use the object.
4. Ask the class to challenge their thinking by visualizing how the object could be used in a different way. For example, the pencil could be used as a balance beam that small plastic animals use to cross a pretend river or lava field. Encourage the children to offer new and creative ideas for how else they might use the object being discussed.
5. Play this game often! It will teach children how to be creative thinkers and problem-solvers when faced with a challenge. Once children understand the activity, apply this concept throughout the year to help children with flexible thinking when they get stuck on doing something or playing in just one way.

Activities to Support Working-Memory Skills

Supporting the development of working-memory skills involves teaching both active listening and how to visualize remembering important information. Engaging children in these types of activities helps them learn how to focus on remembering information they've seen and/or heard and then use that information in social interactions, learning activities, and play.

Activity: What Am I Forgetting?

This is an active-listening activity that helps children with working memory and can be adapted to suit most situations. Think of a situation or routine most children in the class are very familiar with, such as getting ready in the morning, getting ready for bed, or washing their hands. Go over the routine with the children and leave something out. For example, when brushing their teeth, a person opens the tube of toothpaste, squeezes a little onto their toothbrush, turns on the water, holds the brush end of the toothbrush in the water to wet it, turns off the water, brushes their teeth, spits into the sink, rinses the toothbrush, and gets some water to rinse out their mouth. Describe the scene in detail but leave one item out. Encourage children to remember what's been said and to think about what might be missing.

Playing this game regularly will help children with working memory, and over time the skills they learn can be generalized to other classroom activities. Remind the children to think about the activity and the materials they need. Then, they can ask themselves (or be cued by a teacher), "What am I forgetting?"

Intended Outcomes:

- Children will work on active-listening skills.
- Children will develop working-memory skills.
- Children will recognize the importance of remembering everything that's needed to complete tasks and activities.

Materials:

- Optional visuals to support the routine being discussed

What to Do:

1. Gather the children and ask them to sit comfortably because they will be engaging in a visualization activity. Tell them that they will be learning how to listen carefully and use their brains to think up possible answers.
2. Explain that you will describe a well-known activity or routine but that something will be missing. Give an example of this the first few times children engage in this activity so children will know what they should be doing.
3. Remind the children that now it is their turn to think about what has been forgotten. Describe a familiar activity or routine that requires multiple items and leave one out, such as the following.
    - "It's time to get ready for school! I've brushed my teeth and my hair. I ate breakfast. I have on my clothes and my shoes. What am I forgetting?" Possible answers might be lunch, backpack, jacket, or homework.
    - "I'm helping set the table for dinner. I put out plates, napkins, and a spoon and fork for everyone. What am I forgetting?" Possible answers might be cups, food, or water.
4. Restate the list of items when needed if children struggle to remember what's already been listed. Offer hints if children have difficulty coming up with what might be missing.
5. Repeating this activity often will help children improve their skill in making mental lists. Then, when it's time for them to remember the steps needed to complete an activity or the materials that they need, they may be better at remembering what they need to.

Activity: What's Missing?

This is a visual memory activity that helps children improve their visualization and working-memory skills. For this activity, children will be presented with three to six items, such as a toy bus, a blue crayon, a ball, and a plastic bear. They will have time to memorize the objects before they are hidden from view with a towel or blanket. Once hidden, remove one item. Then, show the children the remaining items and ask them to remember which one is missing. Children will train their visual memory skills to recall what items remain and which one is now missing from the group.

Intended Outcomes:

- Children will improve working-memory skills.
- Children will improve visual-memory skills.
- Children will improve sustained attention and focus.

Materials:

- Timer
- Cloth, dish towel, or small blanket
- Three to six different objects

What to Do:

1. Gather children in either a small or large group. This game works well with both sizes as either a center or circle-time activity.
2. Explain to the group that they will look at a group of objects, trying to remember each one. Encourage the children to put a picture of each object into their brain to help them remember what they are seeing.
3. Place three to six objects (fewer objects for younger children) on a table as a center activity or on the carpet as a circle-time activity.
4. Set a timer and give children a minute or two to observe and remember each object. During this time, talk about and label each

item. Emphasize that the children are *looking* and remembering the objects, but they should not touch or move them.

5. When the timer goes off, cover the items with a cloth so they are hidden from view. Before revealing the objects, ask the children to list the items that they saw.
6. Without the children seeing, remove one item from the group. Let the children know that you have taken one object away and when you lift the cloth, they will have to tell you which one it is.
7. Lift the cloth to reveal the objects and encourage the group to state which one is missing.

Playing this game often will improve children's visual memory and visualization skills. These skills support working-memory abilities.

Activities to Support Inhibitory Control

Inhibitory control helps children suppress impulsive reactions so they can stay on task. This helps children use self-control to resist the urge to abandon or lose focus on the task at hand, allowing them to maintain and sustain their attention.

Activities that involve movement, balance, and coordination support inhibitory control skills because they help children remain alert and calm throughout the day. When children regularly engage in movement activities, they are better able to learn, retain information, and control their impulses. Effective movement inputs that can be used in the classroom include the following:

- Dynamic seating
- Balance activities:
  - Walking along a masking-tape balance beam
  - Playing hopscotch
  - Standing-in-place activities

- Movement activities:
    - Freeze Dance
    - Classroom obstacle course
    - Follow the Leader

The following activity teaches children inhibitory control, patience, and active-listening skills in a fun and engaging way.

Activity: Classroom Red Light, Green Light

This game can be played anytime during the school day. Similar to the familiar game, in this version, children stop what they are doing when someone calls out, "Red light!" and then re-engage in what they should be doing when "Green light!" is called out.

Intended Outcomes:

- Children will improve self-control skills.
- Children will inhibit their desire to do something when it isn't the right time.
- Children will improve active-listening skills.

Materials:

- Timer
- Green light visual (optional)
- Red light visual (optional)
- Remaining materials will vary based on the activity

What to Do:

1. Gather the children as a whole group and let them know that they are going to play a game while they work on an activity. Note: You can also play this game during a movement activity; it does not need to be a seated one.

2. Explain that they will be playing classroom Red Light, Green Light and that the purpose of this game is to work on the activity when the leader calls out, "Green light!" and to stop working and wait patiently when the leader calls out, "Red light!" Let the class know that they cannot resume working until the leader calls out, "Green light!"

3. Choose a classroom activity that is repetitive in nature, such as coloring, gluing colorful ripped paper pieces onto cardboard or cardstock, stacking blocks, or sorting manipulatives.

4. Hand out the activity materials.

5. Once everyone understands the rules of the game, call out, "Green light!" so they can begin the activity they should be working on. Let them work for a few minutes.

6. Call out, "Red light!" for them to stop. Praise students for stopping right away and waiting to resume the activity. Then call out, "Green light!" again.

7. Play the game for several minutes, calling out, "Green light!" and "Red light!" periodically. You may wish to choose a new leader from among the children.

8. When the allotted time has ended, talk with the children about the importance of listening and following directions.

Once children understand this game and are proficient at playing it, you can apply the concept throughout the day. For example, if you need to make a special announcement while children are engaged in centers or free play, call out, "Red light!" cueing them to stop whatever they are doing. Make the announcement and then call out, "Green light!" cueing children to go back to what they were doing.

Putting It All Together

Executive function, including attentional flexibility, working memory, and inhibitory control, supports self-regulation by helping children plan, focus, and persist in activities that require sustained attention and control, ultimately enabling them to meet their goals and stay on task. Providing a structured and nurturing environment, developing and posting clear and consistent routines, and engaging in activities that promote executive function skills can help young children develop attention and focus.

Nurturing and developing metacognition skills in children helps them develop strong executive functions, which are crucial for managing tasks, regulating behavior, and problem-solving. Cueing children to access metacognitive thinking before an activity is an effective way to support attention and focus. Children can focus on active listening, improving their working memory, impulse control, and patience.

Playing games that require rule-following, imaginative play, open-ended play, and metacognition is another fun way to develop executive functions. By embedding games and activities that teach flexible thinking, working memory, and inhibitory control into the day, children will build these important skills before they need to use them for successful problem-solving, remembering and completing tasks, adapting to change, and learning new things.

The following chapter will describe the importance of the just right environment, which is made up of physical, social, cultural, and natural elements to support children's ability focus and attend throughout the school day.

Chapter 4
Environmental Considerations to Support Attention and Focus

The environment children learn in affects their energy level, mood, attention, and focus. Think about a time you walked into a store or building and, upon entering, your mood or energy level changed. Maybe you began to feel calmer and more relaxed. Or perhaps the space drained your energy, making you feel tired. You probably enjoy visiting some restaurants more than others. Maybe there are some that you try to avoid because of the way you feel when you eat there. The same is true for children, as the way a space looks, smells, and sounds affects their attention, focus, and energy level. Consider this example highlighting how Ms. Jones designed her first-grade classroom with these elements in mind.

> Ms. Jones has put great effort into creating an environment for herself and her first-grade students that is welcoming, comfortable, and conducive to learning. In addition to designing the space with distinct learning areas, she has taken into account factors such as lighting, air quality, temperature, and noise level. She maximizes the natural light streaming through the windows, which helps prevent the classroom from feeling dim or dreary. On cloudy days, she uses LED lights that mimic daylight as an artificial light source, as they are softer and less harsh than halogen lights.

Ms. Jones strives to maintain a consistent room temperature throughout the day, not too hot or too cold, ensuring she and her students stay focused without feeling sluggish from warmth or distracted by a chilly environment. She also uses an air diffuser, alternating between light citrus and vanilla scents, to keep the air smelling fresh and clean. Avoiding overpowering fragrances, she ensures the classroom smells pleasant but not overwhelming.

To control noise levels, she incorporates noise-dampening elements such as rugs, bean bags, and fabric-covered furniture to absorb sound and reduce distractions. During quiet work sessions, she sometimes plays soft background music or nature sounds to help her students concentrate. The thoughtful balance of light, temperature, noise, and scent allows Ms. Jones and her students to remain comfortable, which in turn enhances their ability to stay focused and engaged throughout the school day.

Physical Environment

The way a space feels, looks, smells, and sounds affects a child's sustained attention and focus. As an effort to support children and their ability to focus on what they should, consider creating a "just right" environment. A just right environment is one that takes into consideration elements such as room temperature, noise level, lighting, clutter, and furniture placement. With some planning and consideration, the classroom environment can look, feel, smell, and sound just right to the majority of children.

Room Temperature

Try to ensure the temperature of the room is comfortable throughout the year. When children are too hot or too cold, they may struggle with attention and focus. Room temperature can impact children's ability to pay attention and focus to the best of their ability. When children feel cold or too warm, their sustained attention and focus diminish because, instead of paying attention to what they should be, their bodies are spending energy trying to warm up or cool down (Haverinen-Shaughnessy and Shaughnessy, 2015). Creating a classroom environment that is at a comfortable temperature throughout the school year will ensure that students are able to dedicate all their mental energy to learning and socializing. Studies show that the optimal classroom temperature to support sustained attention and focus is between 68 and 75 degrees Fahrenheit (Haverinen-Shaughnessy and Shaughnessy, 2015).

Lighting

The light that illuminates a space can affect attention, focus, and energy levels. Studies show that natural light has a positive effect on children's mood, attention in focus, in contrast with artificial lighting (Smolders and de Kort, 2014). Artificial lighting, especially overhead fluorescents, can deplete energy and decrease children's ability to sustain their attention because fluorescent light emits a harsh light that can cause fatigue, eye strain, and loss of focus (Boyce et al., 2006). Here are some tips to improve your classroom's lighting:

- Replace overhead fluorescent light bulbs with LED bulbs. LED bulbs do not emit harsh light like fluorescent lighting does.
- Maximize natural light sources allowing sunlight to illuminate the room as much as possible.
- Keep windows clean and unobstructed. Make sure tall objects, shades, art, and other items are not placed over or in front of windows.
- Unless it is rest time, avoid using heavy drapes, blinds, and shades that block out light.

Room Arrangement

The layout of the early learning environment contributes to how children are able to engage with materials, socialize, learn, and pay attention to what they should be. When teachers create a classroom layout with specific spaces designated for different purposes, children are better able to focus and sustain their attention where it should be. Possible classroom areas might include the following:

- Cozy corner/calm-down corner
- Teacher's area
- Large-group area
- Small-group area
- Learning centers, such as books, blocks, puzzles and games, art exploration, math manipulatives, science exploration, and so on

Consider the following example of how Miss Kay has created a classroom environment that supports attention, engagement, and fosters independence.

> Miss Kay is excited to welcome her prekindergarten children back to the school year. As a veteran teacher, she knows that the layout of an early learning environment contributes to how children engage with materials, socialize, and focus on learning. She's thoughtfully organized her classroom to include several spaces that promote learning, creativity, and a sense of calm. To support her students' ability to pay attention and stay engaged in what they should, Miss Kay has set up five learning spaces. First, she has created a cozy corner. This quiet space is located in the back corner of the room, far away from the front door and carpet area. She has filled the space with soft pillows, plush rugs, and stuffed animals, providing a safe retreat for children who need a break or time to regulate their emotions. She's designated a small teacher's area in the opposite corner of the room where she has a desk and storage cabinet.
>
> In the whole-group area at the front of the room, she has a comfortable chair, a large rug, colorful seating spots for each child, and a whiteboard or interactive display for teaching. This area is where Miss Kay gathers all the children for circle time or group lessons. During group activities, this space helps the children learn how to sit and pay attention while they listen, sing, or participate together. The space

is well-lit, with plenty of natural light streaming in from windows nearby, creating a welcoming atmosphere.

Near the back of the room, Miss Kay has set up small-group learning centers. This designated area has tables and chairs set up for more intimate lessons or one-on-one activities with children. It's a space where Miss Kay can provide targeted instruction or assist children with activities such as preliteracy, early math skills, or open-ended, hands-on projects.

Finally, throughout the room, Miss Kay has set up several learning centers. Each learning center is easily accessible and clearly labeled, enabling the children to independently choose activities that interest them:

- Book center
- Building and construction center
- Imagination play and dress-up center
- Art exploration center
- Science and nature exploration center
- Light table center

By intentionally designing the classroom space with different learning zones, Miss Kay uses the environment as a tool to support her students' attention and focus.

Visual Distractions

Reducing clutter in early learning spaces will decrease unnecessary visual distractions. Highlight children's artwork and finished products and post the daily schedule and class rules at the children's eye level, but try to avoid clutter. When classrooms are clean, organized, and free from too many decorations, children are better able to attend to what they should be because they do not become distracted by the environment. To reduce visual distractions in your classroom, consider these strategies:

- Store toys and learning materials in when not in use.
- Avoid unnecessary furniture and other items in the classroom.

- Use solid-color bins to store toys so children cannot see the contents when they are not in use.
- Label each storage space with a photograph of the contents to make it easier for children to put things away where they belong.
- Arrange furniture with space to move easily between tables, desks, and chairs so it is easy for children to navigate the classroom safely.
- Designate one wall space in the classroom as the spot to hang children's work. The remaining walls should contain only materials that support classroom success, including the class rules and daily routine.
- When possible, place children's work on display on the wall outside the classroom.

Auditory Distractions

When there are fewer auditory distractions, children can concentrate better and sustain their focus without becoming distracted by sounds happening in the environment. Distracting sounds such as loud hallways, noises from outside heard through an open window, coughing and sneezing, and children talking during focused learning time can lead to increased distractibility and impair children's ability to sustain their attention and focus on what they should. To decrease auditory distractions, consider the following:

- Model respectful listening.
- Model using a quiet voice—possibly an "inside voice."
- Place quiet learning areas away from loud hallways and windows.
- Play slow, rhythmic music or white noise during meal and rest time.

Social-Emotional and Cultural Environments

Early learning environments include more than just the physical environment. They are also made up of social, cultural, and natural elements. Together with teaching style and the children in the class, the physical, social, cultural, and natural elements make up a learning environment that is unique and different from any other environment a child may be a part of. The early learning environment often differs significantly from a child's home environment. It's important to discuss this with children, helping them recognize that the values and rules of the class environment are important so they can learn to respect and feel a part of their unique classroom environment. When children feel like they belong and understand that they are an important part of the class as a whole, they tend to be more alert and attentive to the activities happening throughout the day.

Social Environment

Beyond the physical aspects of the environment, an essential social element also plays an important role in early learning environments. The social environment of a classroom refers to the way students perceive their ability to interact with their peers, educators, and caregivers while they engage in learning activities, mealtimes, and free play. When children feel like they belong, are accepted for who they are, and are safe in their environment, they are more apt to participate in class routines and follow the established class rules (Wilkins, Verlenden, Szucs, and Johns, 2022).

To accomplish this, create an environment where positive messaging and language is used both when discussing successes and during times when children's behavior challenges the success or safety of the class.

Develop age-appropriate classroom management techniques and be consistent with following through with these when needed. Create an environment where successes are celebrated and mistakes are recognized as opportunities to learn and grow. Classrooms that are well managed, consistent, and use positive behavior-management strategies help children feel connected to the people around them and the material they are learning (Hawkins et al., 2001). In contrast, classrooms with inconsistent rules and routines and poor behavior-management practices foster confusion and a lack of connectedness for children.

Here are strategies to think about:

- Design classroom activities that are inclusive for all children.
- Have materials that represent the diverse cultures of the children who make up the class.
- Design the classroom so students are able to independently access tools, materials, and activities.
- Develop class rules in child-friendly language. When class rules are broken, use neutral or positive language to remind the child and the class what is acceptable and unacceptable behavior in the class environment.
- Set expectations and boundaries for the class rules and discuss these often as a whole group.
- Post class rules and routines with child-friendly visuals so children can refer to them regularly.

Cultural Environment

Early learning classrooms also have a cultural environment. Classrooms should reflect the diverse backgrounds of the people in them, in terms of ethnicity, culture, language, and abilities. It's important for all children to feel welcome, valued, and comfortable in their classroom. This will foster a deeper connection to learning materials and will help children attend and focus on learning materials and social interactions.

To help all children connect with their learning materials and foster sustained attention and focus, acknowledge the diverse cultural background of the students in a classroom through books, visuals, and materials. This can significantly enhance the learning experience for all students because their unique backgrounds and traditions are valued. When children feel valued and connected to their classroom environment and learning materials, they tend to be more focused and attention to what they are learning.

Consider the following strategies and activities to help all children feel connected and comfortable in their learning spaces:

- Incorporate materials, books, and activities that represent different cultures and perspectives. This could include toys, music, art supplies, and dramatic-play props that reflect a variety of cultures.
- Consider hands-on activities that teach children about different customs, foods, clothing, and celebrations. Activities that resonate with children tend to have a motivational factor that increases attention and focus.
- Read books with characters from diverse backgrounds who represent the ethnic makeup of the classroom. Children are more likely to attend to a story when they "see themselves" on the pages (Dee and Penner, 2017).
- Read books that contain mythical creatures and/or animals. Books with animals and mythical characters are motivating and tend to capture and hold most children's attention.
- Complete home visits and/or invite families into the classroom to share their unique cultural values and traditions.

Children tend to be more engaged and attentive when an activity feels relevant to them. When children see themselves in the materials being used, they tend to be more motivated to engaged and remain attentive to the activity, as illustrated here.

> Mr. Kenan notices that, during story time, some children in his kindergarten class seem disinterested or restless. To address this, he decides to try incorporating books that better reflect the families in his classroom. He chooses *The Proudest Blue: A Story of Hijab and Family* by Ibtihaj Muhammad. This book is about a young girl's older sister—named Asiya—and her first day of wearing a hijab to school. Some of Mr. Kenan's students' family members also wear hijabs. As he begins reading, Mariam, one of his quieter students, sits up straighter and leans in. The rest of the class is equally engaged, fascinated by the colorful illustrations and the story of Asiya's first day wearing a hijab.
>
> Later in the week, Mr. Kenan invites Mariam's family to the classroom to share more about their cultural traditions.

Mariam's mother brings fatteh and saltah, two traditional Yemeni dishes, for the children to taste. The experience not only fosters connection but also encourages the children's attention and focus, as they are excited to learn more about a classmate's culture through both storytelling and food.

Ms. Thompson has been a favorite kindergarten teacher in the same small mountain town in Colorado for almost twenty years. Over time, she has seen the town evolve and its population become increasingly diverse. Today, her kindergarten class is made up of children from a wide range of cultural backgrounds. She understands that teaching young children how to be respectful classmates—how to listen to others' points of view and make positive choices—is an essential part of their development. She's relied on the same books to teach these important skills for many years. This year, however, she has noticed that these books no longer captivate or hold her students' attention. The stories simply aren't resonating with them in the way she hoped. Determined to find a solution, Ms. Thompson replaced her old books with more modern ones that reflect the diversity of her students, such as *My Magical Choices*, part of The Magic of Me series by Becky Cummings. This book, with its vibrant illustrations and empowering message, mirrors the lessons she wants to instill while also representing all the children in her classroom.

From the moment she introduced the book, Ms. Thompson has observed a noticeable shift in the class. Her students were more focused, more attentive, and far more engaged with the story. She has begun incorporating visuals that also represent each of the students in her class to accompany the new books. Again, she has noticed an immediate improvement in her students' focus and attention to the lessons. They have become engaged and interested in the material in the moment, and they have begun applying what they they've learned. By incorporating resources that reflect a variety of backgrounds, she was able to create an environment where each child can see themselves in what they are learning and model that behavior throughout the day.

The Natural Environment and Its Restorative Effect on Attention and Focus

As we've discussed earlier in this book, the amount of time a child can pay attention is limited. This means that a child's ability to attend to a task or activity diminishes or stops altogether when they are required to pay attention for longer than is developmentally appropriate. One way to restore attention is to provide children with frequent breaks throughout the day. Taking breaks in nature, where children have access to green space, will help them refocus on classroom activities. A green space, refers to man-made area that is designed for recreation and relaxation, such as a large lawn, park, or garden. There is evidence suggesting that when children leave the classroom environment and enter a green space even for a few minutes, they are more ready to learn, socialize, and retain information (Vanaken and Danckaerts, 2018; van Oordt, Ouwehand, and Paas, 2022). Following is an example of how Ms. Miller uses a local green space to help her students regain their ability to focus and pay attention in the classroom.

> Ms. Miller has just started working as a first-grade teacher in an urban public school. Before this, she taught in a rural community in New England. There, she and her students frequently benefited from learning outdoors, as the school was surrounded by a forest. At her new school, the students have access to a playground but, aside from a small garden the upper classes maintain, there is little green space for children to explore. One morning, in late September, after a few hours of beginning-of-the-year testing, Ms. Miller notices that her students are restless and are starting to lose focus. She tries to gather the class to the rug to listen to stories, but some are easily distracted while others are unable to sit still. She decides it's time for a quick break and takes the students to a nearby community park, just a short walk away. She'd already inquired about taking the class to visit this park and has received approval from the children's caregivers.

As they step outside, the change is immediate. When the class arrives at the park, the busy city sounds fade and are replaced by the chatter of nearby squirrels and the occasional car passing in the distance. The children are surrounded by nothing but green space complete with trees, bushes, and flowering plants. At first, the children are curious but a bit hesitant, unsure about the park since it's not a place they often visit as a class. But as they start to explore, they find new things to look at. Some students spot a tree with colorful leaves, and others notice the flowers blooming along the path. A few children are intrigued by a couple of pigeons pecking at the ground. Ms. Miller guides the class to a small grassy area, encouraging them to sit and relax. She invites the children to take a deep breath and listen to the different sounds around them, helping them tune into the calm of the moment. A student points out a butterfly fluttering by, and another notices a patch of grass growing through a crack in the sidewalk. After about fifteen minutes in the park, the children feel more connected to their environment. They've had a chance to run around, stretch their legs, and just be present in this natural space.

Back in the classroom, Ms. Miller notices that her students are noticeably calmer, more focused, and eager to dive into their next activity. The time outdoors in the park, even for a short while, helped them restore their ability to focus making it easier for them to return to learning with more attention and energy. Throughout the year, Ms. Miller and her first-grade class continue to visit the park whenever they need time to recharge and refocus.

Green spaces could include playgrounds, school yards, and nature walks where children are exposed to trees, shrubs, grass, birdsong, breezes, and sunlight. Transitioning out of the classroom into nature or a green space provides young children with an opportunity to experience a break from the usual sights, sounds, and expectations of the classroom. This break in a natural environment has a restorative effect on children's attention and focus.

In the following example, Ms. Lynda, a Head Start teacher, uses the school's community garden space to help restore attention and focus with her preschoolers.

> Ms. Lynda's preschool class has had a difficult few days maintaining focus and attention during circle and mealtimes. Two of her students, Marcus and Jace, often struggle to sit still and pay attention during these parts of the day. This week, a few other children are also having trouble staying quiet and engaged during snack and circle time. One morning, instead of transitioning directly to circle time and centers, Ms. Lynda decides it's time for a short break outside. The class heads to the school garden, where they're surrounded by small trees, flowers, and vegetables growing in containers. Immediately, the natural surroundings capture their attention, especially Marcus and Jace. Ms. Lynda points to a bird perched on a branch, then shows them the tomatoes and peppers growing. To everyone's delight, a bunny scurries by and hides in the bushes. Ms. Lynda notices the children are excited and engaged with the plants and animals around them.
>
> After a short while, they transition back to the classroom and sit down on the rug for circle time. Ms. Lynda brings with her a stick, a green leaf, and one of the ripe peppers. She uses these items to engage the class and encourages the children to share what they remember seeing and hearing. Jace excitedly reminds the class about the bunny they saw, and Marcus describes the plants that were growing. All of the children are eager to share, ask insightful questions, and talk about the plants and creatures they encountered. After spending just fifteen minutes outdoors, Ms. Lynda notices that the children are calmer and more focused in classroom. The outdoor time not only helped them regain focus but also sparked their curiosity and sense of wonder.

There is strong evidence suggesting that when children spend time, even for brief periods, in nature, their ability to attend to school activities improves when they return to the classroom. In nature, they take a break from the usual sights, sounds, and stimuli in their learning environments.

When they return to the classroom, children's attention and ability to focus is replenished and restored (van Oordt, Ouwehand, and Paas, 2022). A theory called the attention restoration theory (ART) suggests that people are better at concentrating after they have spent time in nature (Kaplan and Kaplan, 1989). This theory asserts that when people are able to take a mental break from the demands and usual distractions of a learning space in nature, their attention is renewed and restored (Kaplan and Kaplan, 1989; Kaplan, 1995).

When children take breaks in nature, they are not just distancing themselves from the physical classroom but also from the intense mental effort involved in processing information, following instructions, and paying attention. In a classroom setting, children are constantly engaged with multiple stimuli, including their peers, lessons, and classroom rules. These demands can lead to cognitive fatigue, which makes it harder to maintain focus for extended periods of time. Green spaces and nature can provide students with a break from the sensory stimuli associated with a classroom—such as bright lights, noise, and learning materials. Breaks in nature incorporate movement, whether it's walking, running, or exploring. This combination of exposure to nature with movement can help children regulate emotions, reduce impulsivity, and improve overall sustained attention and focus. With this in mind, consider the following to help children benefit from the restorative power of taking brain breaks.

- Limit the length of time children engage in learning activities based on age.
- Expose children to green spaces daily. These might be walks through a community garden, a walk around a tree-lined block, or exploring a green space created inside the building (such as an atrium or indoor garden filled with potted plants). The restorative effect of nature on attention is directly related to green spaces, not just being outdoors.
- Design lessons that can occur outdoors when time and weather permit.

Putting It All Together

The environment has a significant effect on children's attention span. A learning environment that supports attention and focus is one that minimizes distractions, creates a positive social environment, and uses culturally relevant materials. Developing consistent classroom rules and routines, creating lessons that last only as long as a child's attention span, and providing frequent breaks will help ensure that all children are able to focus and attend throughout the day. Children feel valued and connected to the learning materials and content, which contributes to improved attention and focus.

The next chapter will discuss simple and effective sensory-based strategies that can be used throughout the day to further support children's sustained attention and focus.

Chapter 5
Sensory Inputs, Games, and Strategies to Support Attention and Focus

When an activity is interesting to children, they are more likely to interact and engage with it. Sensory inputs can be used to enhance most, if not all, learning activities. Sensory inputs, games, and strategies are designed to help children focus, regulate their emotions, and maintain an optimal level of arousal. A wide variety of objects and activities, including movement, fidget toys, visual timers, and noise-canceling headphones, can serve as sensory tools. In addition, inputs that stimulate children's senses increase children's curiosity, interest, and motivation.

For example, during a lesson in which children are learning to count, consider using a manipulative such as small plastic bears or pompoms for children to count. Or at circle time, when talking about the rain forest, pass around colorful bird feathers, safe live plants or fake replicas, and toy animals that live in the rainforest. While teaching letter formation, provide opportunities for children to practice forming letters and lines in shaving cream, colorful sand, or fingerpaint. When a learning environment is rich with multisensory inputs, children are more motivated to focus and sustain their attention on what they should be learning.

This chapter explores four types of sensory inputs that are effective at supporting children's sustained attention and focus in early learning environments: tactile, auditory, visual, and movement. The tactile system is responsible for the sense of touch. When used as a sensory tool, tactile inputs may help increase children's interest and engagement in activities. The auditory system is responsible for the sense of sound. When used as a sensory tool, auditory inputs support a calm and peaceful classroom environment. The visual system is responsible for the sense of sight. When used as a sensory tool, visual inputs can enhance a learning activity to help children sustain their attention and remain focused on the activity. Visual sensory input is also used to calm children who are feeling overwhelmed or dysregulated. Movement input, guided by the vestibular system, is responsible for balance and sensing movement. The vestibular system detects head movement, gravity, and acceleration, sending signals to the brain that help people understand where they are in space (Ayres, 1972). Movement activities stimulate this system and can help children improve their sustained attention and focus (May-Benson and Koomar, 2010). When used as a sensory tool, movement inputs can also help children attain and maintain an alert and calm level of arousal throughout the day.

Arousal Level

In addition to helping children focus and engage with learning activities, sensory inputs can have a positive effect on arousal levels. *Arousal level* refers to how alert and attentive a person is at a given moment. An optimal level of arousal is one in which children are alert and focused and their energy level aligns with the activities they are participating in. For example, during rest time, children's arousal level should be low so they can remain calm and quiet. When rest time ends, children's arousal level should rise to match the demands of the next activity. During free-choice time, children should have an arousal level that is both alert and calm so they can interact with activities and other children to the best of their ability.

A variety of sensory strategies can help children adjust their arousal level to the activity or situation they are participating in. Chapter 4 explored ways to develop a classroom environment that is "just right" for optimal attention and focus. Arousal level can be thought about in a similar way. It is important that children have a "just right" level of arousal—one that is not too high or too low so they are able to focus and sustain their attention throughout the day. With this in mind, note that some children will benefit from sensory strategies that decrease their arousal level, while others will benefit from inputs that make them more alert and engaged. Even during the same lesson, some children may need help to calm down while others may need support to become more alert and increase their arousal level. Consider the following example that describes the attention and focus challenges Ms. Jeffries faces during large-group instruction.

> Ms. Jeffries gathers her kindergarteners together on the carpet whenever she introduces new material to the class. She wants to make sure everyone learns about new topics at the same time. A few of her students have difficulty paying attention. Some can't sit still. They roll around on the carpet and distract the children sitting close to them. Other children in the group seem bored and disengaged in what she is explaining. Each of these behaviors is challenging for Ms. Jeffries to manage while she introduces new learning material. Both types of behaviors suggest that the arousal level of the students is not optimal for engaging with and paying attention to what she is teaching. The children who cannot sit still would benefit from inputs to decrease their arousal level. In contrast, the students who seem bored would benefit from inputs to increase their arousal level.

Tactile Games, Activities, and Inputs to Support Attention, Focus, and Arousal Level

The tactile sensory system is responsible for the sense of touch. Used as a sensory tool, tactile inputs can be used in early learning environments to improve children's motivation. Tactile inputs help children engage with and remain focused on the activity at hand, improve their sustained attention, and remain motivated to participate in established class routines. Tactile inputs that support an alert and calm level of arousal include fidget toys, manipulatives, tactile sensory play, and messy tactile activities.

Fidget Toys

A fidget toy is a small object a child can easily hold in their hand and fidget with during sedentary seated activities such as circle time or listening to a story. Many people fidget as a means to stay mentally alert and focused. Some people may twirl their hair, tap their fingers, or play with a pen or pencil. These movements are small and nondisruptive, unlike large body movements such as getting up and leaving an activity, rolling around on the floor, or bothering a peer. Allowing children to engage with fidget toys will not only decrease large, disruptive fidgeting, but will also support children while they sit and pay attention to a lesson or story. Popular and effective fidget toys include fidget cubes, fidget spinners, stress balls, and bubble fidgets such as Pop Its.

How to Use Fidget Toys

The purpose of a fidget toy is to help a child attain and then sustain an alert and calm arousal level. These toys can diminish distracting restless energy during seated learning activities. Here are some ways to get the most out of fidget toys:

- Provide children with a variety of fidget toys. Place the toys in an open container, giving children easy access to choose what looks right to them.

- At the start of a seated learning activity, allow each child to pick a fidget toy. It is okay if a child refuses to take a toy. Discourage children from taking more than one fidget.

- Remind children of the established rules about how to use fidget toys correctly. Key points for establishing rules to correctly using fidget toys might include the following:

    ○ **Use when necessary:** Fidget toys should be used to help children maintain their focus, not as a way to avoid work or participation.

> Encourage children to use them only when they feel they need help staying calm or focusing.
>
> - **Set boundaries:** Introduce fidgets as a tool to use for focusing and paying attention, not a toy for playing with. Describe that it's okay to squeeze or spin a fidget toy quietly, but it's not okay to make noise with it or use it to distract others.
>
> - **Monitor usage:** Adults should check in to ensure the child isn't relying on the fidget toy too much or using it as an excuse to avoid tasks.
>
> - **Choose nondistracting items as fidgets:** Offer quiet, tactile toys that don't make noise or draw attention to themselves, as this can disrupt others around them.
>
> - Using fidget toys in a purposeful way helps children stay focused on what they should be and helps them build skills to maintain their attention independently. Begin the learning activity and allow children to interact with their fidget toy as they want to (as long as it is not distracting).
>
> - At the conclusion of the activity, put out the fidget container so children can put their fidget away. Remind children the fidget toys will be available the next time they need one.

Fidget toys are not useful when children are more actively engaged in a learning activity. During active learning, a fidget toy would distract children from what they should be engaging with. Instead, when children are actively engaged in a learning activity, consider enhancing the activity with a relevant manipulative.

Manipulatives

A manipulative is a physical item a child can engage with. Manipulatives make learning hands-on, which can improve engagement, attention, and focus. For example, use coins, pompoms, or small plastic bears when working on counting and basic math skills. Instead of plain paper, provide chalk and sandpaper for children to use for writing lines and letters. The scratchy texture of the sandpaper will provide children with enhanced feedback when they write on it using chalk. Work on letter identification by having children search for Scrabble or Bananagrams letters hidden in sand or shredded paper.

Tactile Sensory Play

Tactile sensory play involves activities that engage a child's sense of touch. This type of play helps develop fine-motor skills, coordination, and cognitive abilities. It also encourages creativity and exploration, offering a hands-on learning experience that can be alerting and calming for children. When children interact with materials with an alert and calm state of mind, they are better able to sustain their attention and focus. Tactile sensory play is open-ended, hands-on play that helps children learn motor, language, and social skills. Open-ended play has no set end point or right way to engage in the activity; instead, children succeed simply by engaging. Open-ended play fosters creativity, critical thinking, and problem-solving skills and encourages children to explore and engage with materials and ideas in their own unique ways. This allows children to get creative and use their imaginations and promotes independence, problem-solving skills, and confidence while providing opportunities to improve fine- and gross-motor skills through process-based, rather than product-based, interactions. Examples of open-ended tactile play materials include:

- Blocks and magnetic tiles for building and constructing
- Loose parts such as buttons, stones, scraps of fabric, or recycled materials for building and constructing
- Sensory bins filled sand, water, slime, shredded paper, and so on
- Art materials such as playdough, fingerpaint, and kinetic sand

> Jesse is a six-year-old student repeating kindergarten at his local public school. Last year, he attended a small

private kindergarten where his teachers recommended repeating the grade due to difficulties with consistent letter recognition and identification. This year, his teacher, Ms. Lindsey, has noticed that Jesse is patient, thoughtful, and eager to learn—except during the early literacy block. During this time, he becomes easily distracted and shows little interest in writing, letter identification, or developing basic writing skills. He often leaves his seat and becomes upset when asked to do his work. Ms. Lindsey believes Jesse could benefit from a more process-oriented, open-ended approach to developing early literacy skills. To support this, she creates a small sensory bin filled with colored sand and hides capital letters inside. She adds a dinosaur-head gripper and encourages Jesse to use it to search for and grasp the letters. She sets out sandpaper, chalk, and playdough and invites all the students to practice letter formation with these materials. She demonstrates how they can find letters in the sensory bin and form them on the sandpaper using chalk or playdough. Jesse, along with his classmates, immediately engages in these tactile activities. He shows improved sustained attention to these interactive tasks and attempts to identify and form letters on his own. By offering an open-ended, tactile approach to letter recognition, Ms. Lindsey has provided Jesse with engaging activities to improve his skills without becoming overly frustrated or inattentive.

Messy Tactile Activities

Don't be afraid to let children get messy while they learn. When children engage in messy play activities such as sand and water tables, fingerpaint, or playdough, they develop social skills, impulse control, and patience. In addition, messy play is exciting and interesting for most young children, so adding a messy tactile component to learning activities can improve sustained attention and focus. In this vignette, Mr. Rivers makes some changes to the way he approaches early literacy by integrating tactile activities and is pleasantly surprised at the outcome.

Mr. Rivers's prekindergarten class is made up of a lively group of four- and five-year-olds. He's noticed that, right from the start, they work well as a group. With the exception of the early literacy activities, they also participate in all of the classroom routines well. During early literacy learning, many of the children struggle to sustain their attention on Mr. Rivers's worksheets. Since his students do not seem to struggle in other parts of the day, he decides to make some changes to the way he is teaching early literacy. Mr. Rivers tapes long pieces of butcher paper on each table. He puts out watercolors and fingerpaints and encourages his students to draw, scribble, and form letters and numbers on the paper.

The next day, he works on letter identification and matching by hiding capital letters in sand and having students write the letters they find in shaving cream. Later in the week, he works on letter formation by having children write with chalk on sandpaper. Finally, he puts out modeling clay and encourages his students to roll out the clay, separate it into lines, and then form capital letters and shapes with it. By adding in messy tactile inputs, Mr. Rivers has captivated his students' attention during early literacy learning. The children are excited to participate in these activities, and Mr. Rivers notices that everyone's sustained focus and attention immediately improves.

A sensory bin is a useful tool that can be used during free-choice time, outdoor play, or during center learning. A large sensory bin such as a sand and water table can be a feature out on the playground or in a preschool classroom in an area where the floor is easy to clean. Small sensory bins such as baking sheets or small plastic containers may provide individual interaction during centers and seated learning. Regularly cleaning and switching out the base material and the filler items will keep children interested and motived to interact with the sensory bin. In the following example, Charlie's teacher, Ms. Henries, uses sensory bins to help improve her attention and focus during drawing and writing activities.

Charlie is a bright and energetic four-and-a-half-year-old. She enjoys preschool and usually is an active participant in activities. However, she dislikes drawing and writing; whenever the class works on these activities, Charlie seems to be uninterested. Often, she abandons the activity before it ends, and Ms. Henries attempts to redirect her back to the activity. Ms. Henries has observed that Charlie's drawing skills are far below the rest of the class. Ms. Henries realizes that Charlie may have little interest in drawing and writing because her skills are not strong in this area. So, she decides to incorporate an individual sensory bin for Charlie when it is time to work on letter formation. She gives Charlie and a group of her peers baking trays filled with colored sand. Ms. Henries demonstrates how they can practice writing letters in the sand with their fingers. For the first time, Charlie sits and pays attention to the activity for the full learning block. She tries her best to form each of the letters Ms. Henries calls out.

During centers, Ms. Henries has set up a large sensory bin filled with shredded paper and plastic and foam letters. She shows the class that they can search through the shredded paper for different letters and, when they find one, they can think about what letter they've found. When it's Charlie's turn for this center activity, she is alert and focused and fully engages for the entire amount of time. Both of these activities directly address early literacy skills, ones Charlie typically avoids. But because they are interesting and hands-on, Charlie is engaged and attentive.

Activity: Learning with Sensory Bins

A sensory bin is a container that allows children to play and interact with materials with their hands. Sensory bins are specifically designed provide an open-ended play and learning experience. A large bin allows multiple children to engage in the same activity at the same time. A small bin, such as a baking tray or metal pie plate, is perfect for individual play.

The base material in a sensory bin might include something dry that will not stick to a child's hands, or it can be wet and messy. Dry materials to consider include the following:

- Pompoms
- Shredded paper
- Colored sand
- Small rocks

Wet materials to consider include the following:

- Water
- Shaving cream
- Fingerpaint
- Slime

Once you have chosen the base material, add items for children to interact with. These might be kitchen utensils and pretend food options to work on self-help skills. You might include plastic letters to work on letter identification and early literacy skills. Or you could include plastic bugs, farm animals, or mythical creatures to encourage pretend play. Add these items to the base and the bin is ready for children to explore, learn, play, and improve their skills!

Visual Inputs to Support Attention, Focus, and Arousal Level

Visual sensory inputs may be used in a variety of ways to support children's alert and calm level of arousal. Children can engage in visual activities when they are overly excited, upset, or frustrated. Visual aids may also be used to support classroom management skills, foster independence, and help children pay attention to what they should be. This section describes how visual sensory inputs can help children regulate their arousal levels, supporting them when they are overly excited, upset, or frustrated, while also enhancing classroom management, fostering independence, and improving attention to tasks.

Calming Visual Inputs

Visual inputs that have a calming effect on children's regulation and arousal level include toys that provide slow, flowing movement for children to watch, such as the following:

- Sand timers
- Glitter jars
- Liquid motion toys
- Sensory tubes

Watching slow movement is soothing to children, so these toys have a calming effect on arousal level and regulation. Additionally, when children interact with soothing visual inputs, they engage in a calm, purposeful activity that gives them time calm down and regulate their emotions. The following example highlights how Jakari's preschool teacher, Ms. Fishburn, helps him regulate his emotions using calming visual input.

> Jakari's emotions often get the better of him throughout the day. He is a kind and sensitive three-year-old who really struggles to remain calm and in control of his emotions, especially at drop-off in the morning. He is still learning how to separate from his parents, and the transition to the classroom is often challenging for him. Ms. Fishburn tries to help Jakari calm down, but she also needs to greet the rest of the children and talk with caregivers. She would like him to engage in something meaningful and purposeful each morning, but he is usually too upset to play on his own or with a peer.
>
> One morning, she brings in a moving sand-art picture she received as a gift. She places it on a shelf in a quiet corner of the room and, when Jakari comes to class, she walks him over to it. She shows him how to turn the frame upside down

to shift the sand and water. As Jakari engages with the item, he slowly calms down and regains control of his emotions. Later in the week, with Jakari in mind, Ms. Fishburn introduces other slow-motion toys to the whole class. Soon, the room is filled with slow-motion visual items, including sand timers and glitter jars. Ms. Fishburn has created a visually soothing space with multiple opportunities to interact with calming toys. Jakari can access these items throughout the classroom, helping him calm down more quickly after he transitions into the classroom each morning.

Visual Aids

Post important visual aids, such as classroom rules, the class routine, and other common daily routines such as handwashing, using the bathroom, and transitions. The thoughtful use and placement of visual aids in an early learning environment can act as a support for children's ability to sustain their attention and focus on what they need to. Common visuals can include the following:

- Daily schedule (with images for preliterate children)
- Classroom rules
- Classroom management tips:
    - Voice volume chart
    - Calm-down strategies
    - Positive behavior supports
- Visual aids for common routines:
    - Handwashing
    - Transitioning from home to school
    - Using the bathroom

Visual Organization

Many young children have difficulty ignoring exciting visuals, desired toys, and other visual distractions when these items are in plain sight.

As noted in chapter 4, a neat and tidy classroom is the optimal learning environment to support students as they focus and attend to what they should.

Projects and artwork are the most common items that create a cluttered and distracting visual environment. To cut down on the distractions, consider designating one space in the classroom to post children's creations. If possible, post additional artwork outside the classroom in the hallway. To further reduce clutter, try to send completed schoolwork and art projects home daily.

Use solid-colored bins to store toys, games, and learning materials when they are not in use. This will keep the class organized. Solid-colored bins decrease visual distractions because children cannot see the contents when the items are not in use. Bins should be clearly labeled with photos and words to show the children what belongs inside.

Consider the following example describing how Ms. Henries supports one of her students who becomes easily distracted.

> Dylan, a peer of Jakari's in Ms. Henries's class, is an energetic three-and-a-half-year-old. He loves dinosaurs, especially the large triceratops in the play area. Each day, children enter the room and have time for free play before they sit down for breakfast. Dylan has difficulty transitioning from the play area to the table because he doesn't want to stop playing with the dinosaurs. Most mornings, he refuses to put the triceratops down and brings it to the table with him. When other children see that he's brought a toy to the table, they want to do the same, which disrupts mealtime. Ms. Henries encourages children to clean up the play area, but there isn't a designated space for everything. Instead, children place the items they played with on open shelves. The shelves are visible from the table, so the children are distracted from what they should be focusing on. Ms. Henries wants to stop children from bringing toys to the table and decides that a new clean-up routine might help. She purchases large, solid-colored bins. She labels each bin with a photograph of the items that should be placed in

each one. She shows the bins to the children and explains which toys belong in each one. She lets the children know that when it is time to clean up, the toys get put in the bins so they don't get lost.

Later in the day, when free time ends, Dylan doesn't want to put the triceratops in the bin. Ms. Henries lets him know that the bin is the dinosaur's home and he needs to go home for a while to rest. She assures him that the triceratops will be there when it is time for free play again. Then, she shows him on the visual schedule when that will happen next in the day.

On the first day with this new clean-up system, Dylan has difficulty accepting this change, but by the end of the week he is transitioning to mealtime with no toy in hand. Ms. Henries has created a new clean-up routine to support children's attention and focus during mealtimes. By removing toys from her students' line of vision, they are more inclined to focus on what they should be doing. Further, she uses the visual schedule to help Dylan understand when he can play with the dinosaurs throughout the day.

Auditory Inputs to Support Attention, Focus, and Arousal Level

Auditory sensory inputs help set the mood and tone of the classroom. A loud classroom with poor acoustics might make students feel overly excited and overstimulated. Their voice levels will increase to match the decibel level of the classroom. A quiet classroom with calm music encourages the students to remain calm and in control of their emotions and actions.

Music can soothe students during challenging parts of the day. Slow, rhythmic music played when students enter the classroom in the morning, during meals, and during rest times may help children regulate their nervous systems to better handle their emotions (Shield and Dockrell, 2008).

Control the Noise Level of the Classroom

A classroom can become loud because children's voice levels are loud. When this happens, it may be hard for young children to focus on what they should. The following are strategies to help children lower their voice volume.

Post a voice level chart in the classroom. Describe what each volume sounds like and how children can change their voices to match each level. For example, the quietest level means no talking. The second quietest means whispering. The loudest level means talking and laughing as loud as one wants to and may be right for outside play. Practice voice volume as a class activity so that children know what to do when you cue them to decrease the noise level in the class. Model how to talk in a quiet voice. Talking in a calm and quiet voice encourages children to do the same.

Use a signal to cue children to stop, look, and listen. This might be hand clap, banging a drum or gong, or a simple chant such as, "One, two, three, eyes on me." A cue alerts the children to reset the voice volume in the room and to use a quieter voice.

Decrease Auditory Distractions

Auditory distractions might include a chatty classmate, children with allergies who sneeze and sniffle frequently, birds chirping outdoors, noisy fans and heaters, or people talking in the hallway. These distractions affect sustained and selective attention because they draw the attention away from something relevant to what has caused the sound.

Background noises are distracting and, when possible, should be eliminated to help support children's attention. When auditory distractions cannot be eliminated, consider these strategies.

To decrease distractions from the hallway, keep the classroom door closed. Or, close the hallway door during high-traffic times of the day. To limit distractions from noises in the classroom, play white noise during quiet parts of the day. Place furniture away from loud heaters, windows, and doors.

Movement Inputs to Support Attention, Focus, and Arousal Level

When the day offers children regular opportunities to exercise and move their bodies, they will be more able to learn and retain information. Movement input is a powerful sensory tool to help children calm their bodies and restless energy. Movement can have an alerting as well as a calming effect on children who have difficulty with attention, focus, and distractibility. Movement's effects on supporting an alert and calm level of arousal last for a period of time after children have stopped the movement activity (May-Benson and Koomar, 2010). The more children participate in movement activities, the better they can attend and focus during sedentary activities such as mealtime, circle time, or seated activities.

Balance activities engage the vestibular system and help children improve focus and attention. These activities can easily be incorporated into the day during moments when children are waiting in line, transitioning between activities, or between lessons. Simple balance activities include the following:

- Balancing on one foot: This activity requires focus and concentration, helping children feel more grounded and improving their ability to concentrate.
- Walking on a balance beam or a tape line on the floor: This activity encourages focus by requiring children to concentrate on their movements and spatial awareness.
- Yoga poses: Poses such as the tree pose or child's pose stimulate the vestibular system while promoting focus and calmness.

Games that involve movement, especially those that require direction changes or varying speeds, can also stimulate the vestibular system.

Examples include the following:

- Simon Says: Play Simon Says in the classroom or on the playground, making sure to incorporate movements such as spinning, jumping, or crawling during the game. This can activate the vestibular system and help children focus and attend.
- Obstacle courses: Develop simple obstacle courses in the classroom that involve navigating over, under, and around classroom objects.

By incorporating short, frequent, vestibular-stimulating activities throughout the school day, teachers can support children's ability to focus and regulate attention, ultimately creating a more productive and engaging learning environment.

Incorporate Movement Input throughout the Day

Provide opportunities for movement in two- to ten-minute intervals each hour throughout the day—but especially before circle time, mealtimes, and seated work. Movement opportunities between more sedentary times in the day will support them while they sit and sustain their attention and focus. Here are simple ideas to add movement into the day:

During transitions:

- Have children line up on a "balance beam" made of colored masking tape on the floor in front of the door. As they prepare to leave the classroom, encourage them to walk along the tape, focusing on maintaining their balance and staying on the line as they move.
- Make a hopscotch board with masking tape on the floor in the hallway outside the classroom. Invite the children to hopscotch out into the hallway and line up.
- Encourage children to try to balance on one foot as they wait to transition out of the classroom.

While waiting for a guest speaker to arrive or meals to be delivered:

- Gather children on the carpet and play Freeze Dance.

- Have children stand at a safe distance from one another and play the game Simon Says.
- Try out and hold basic yoga poses such as downward dog, cat-cow, or tree pose.

Before seated activities:

- Provide a balance between seated activities and movement. Young children can only sit and pay attention for two to ten minutes at a time, depending on their ages. After that, it is normal for their attention and focus to diminish.
- Spend one to three minutes before seated learning activities engaging in some type of organized movement input such as:
    - Yoga poses
    - Freeze Dance
    - Hopping or jumping in place

Incorporate Movement into Learning Activities

There are times when it is not possible for children to engage in a movement activity before a seated learning activity. Adding a movement component during learning activities will help children stay focused and attentive. Consider these possibilities:

- During early literacy learning, invite children to get up and search the classroom for objects that begin with a specific letter or sound. For example, when learning about the letter *B*, children may search the room and find a bear, blocks, or a ball.
- When learning about sounds, cue children with a sound and then encourage them to find something that sounds similar. For example, when children are working on learning the *D* sound, they might locate a desk, a toy dog, or a dinosaur.
- When learning to count, encourage children to hop or jump on one foot as they work on their counting skills.

Putting It All Together

A classroom rich with tactile, visual, auditory, and movement inputs will help learners sustain their attention so they can focus on what they should be all day long. Embedding sensory activities and supports into the school day will help children prepare to focus and attend throughout the day. Adding tactile and visual inputs to learning activities make activities more interesting. Intentionally posting relevant visual aids and creating a calm and soothing auditory environment helps children attain and maintain an alert and calm level of arousal. Encouraging hands-on learning and messy tactile play improves engagement, sustained attention, and focus. Making sure children have regular opportunities to move their bodies, whether it be free play outside or more organized movement such as Freeze Dance or yoga, will help children maintain an optimal arousal level.

The next chapter highlights specific ways to teach young children what to pay attention to, and how to sustain their attention for an age-appropriate amount of time. The chapter explores listening games, visual activities, and metacognition to teach children attention and focusing skills.

Chapter 6
Educational Games and Activities to Teach and Encourage Focus and Concentration

Early learning classrooms are excellent environments for teaching children how to focus and pay attention. By creating a positive learning environment that incorporates games and activities targeted at teaching children how to focus and pay attention, educators can foster an environment that teaches and nurtures these important skills.

Developing short, highly engaging activities will help ensure that children are able to sustain their attention for the duration of the activity. As a reminder, children's attention spans last for brief amounts of time, depending on their ages:

- Two-year-olds: four to six minutes
- Three-year-olds: six to eight minutes
- Four-year-olds: eight to twelve minutes
- Five- to six-year-olds: ten to eighteen minutes

When developing learning blocks and activities, it is important to consider the average age of the children in the class because this correlates with attention span. A lesson for a group of toddlers should last for a maximum of five to six minutes; an activity geared for five-year-olds may last up to fifteen minutes. This is especially important to remember in mixed-age classrooms, as the attention span of a new three-year-old may be half the time of their five-year-old classmate.

Through consistent classroom management, metacognitive thinking, and educational games, young children can learn how to focus, sustain their attention, and demonstrate good selective attention. Embed these strategies into the classroom to support children as they learn how to focus and pay attention.

Positive Supports

Consistent and positive classroom management includes using praise as appropriate, rewarding children's focus and attention, and creating a positive learning environment.

Praise

Praise children for good listening, strong focus, and sustained attention. Highlight examples of children who demonstrated good focus and attention. For example, compliment a student who stuck with an activity even when it was hard for them. Or, describe that you witnessed many students sustaining their focus on their work instead of talking with a neighbor or walking around the classroom.

Reward Focus and Attention

Create a reward system that highlights when children exhibit sustained attention to a task or activity, good focus, or strong concentration skills. Consider using a sticker chart to highlight when children in the class demonstrate good focus and attending skills. An alternative is to place a pompom in a jar each time any child in the class shows good attention or focus. When the chart or jar are full, hold a celebration to highlight how good the class is at focus and attention.

Create a Supportive Learning Environment

Create a learning environment that helps children attend and focus to the best of their ability. Strategies include the following:

- Breaking down multistep activities into smaller parts

- Following consistent rules and routines
- Using consistent behavior-management techniques

When children know what to expect throughout the day, they are better at sticking with an activity.

Metacognition

Metacognition, the awareness of one's own thought process, refers to how people think about the way they think. When children begin to understand their own thinking processes, they become more independent learners. Encouraging children to think about how they think is a powerful way to help children take ownership of their learning by actively monitoring and adjusting their strategies, rather than relying solely on the teacher to remind them to focus or pay attention.

Activity: Activating the Senses

Teaching young children to visualize their senses and understand which senses they use when they listen and remember can improve their active listening and working-memory skills. Young children need to learn that their ears listen and their eyes see. When they think about these senses and learn how to intentionally access them, children learn that listening, looking, and remembering are important. Children can learn to "activate" their senses when they are cued to do so.

Intended Outcomes:

- Children will learn what their senses are used for.
- Children will think about using their ears to listen.
- Children will think about using their eyes to look and focus on what they need to.
- Children will actively think about remembering what they need to.
- Children will demonstrate increased awareness of the importance of listening and remembering.

Materials:

- Visual of a pair of eyes
- Visual of an ear
- Visual of a brain

What to Do:

1. Present the class with a visual of an ear, and ask the children what they use their ears for. If needed, remind them that they use their ears to listen to directions.
2. Present a visual of a pair of eyes. Ask the class what they use their eyes for. Remind children that they need to use their eyes to see what they are doing, look for materials, and copy actions.
3. Show the class a visual of a brain, and ask what people use their brains for. Cue the children that they can use their brains to remember the steps to complete an activity.

It may take young children a few learning opportunities to remember what the eyes, ears, and brain are for. This is an activity that the teacher can repeat often until everyone in the class understands.

Later, when the class understands how they use their eyes, ears, and brains to help them learn, focus, and pay attention, cue children that they will need to use these senses before starting a learning activity. At the start of a new activity, teach children that listening and remembering are important skills and that their eyes, ears, and brain help them with these skills.

To cue children to activate their senses before a learning activity begins, use upbeat, child-friendly language such as, "Okay, this is important. Time to tell your brain to remember what I am saying." Or, "Time for listening and learning! Let's turn on our listening ears!"

Educational Games and Activities That Teach Attention

There are many games and activities that can teach and encourage attention and focusing skills in young children. Playing these games regularly will help children develop and improve their attention span, sustained attention, and selective attending skills. Popular visual searching games, such as I Spy or Spot It, help children improve selective attention skills. Listening games such as Bingo improve selective and sustained attention skills. Sorting activities also improve these skills.

Visual Activities

Good attention helps people focus on the details of an activity. Look-and-find visual activities, such as the following, encourage the development of this skill.

- Where's Waldo?
- I Spy books or apps
- Spot It
- Hidden Pictures
- Spot the Difference

These are activities that one child can complete or a small group can engage in during small-group time or as a center activity. Remember that young children may only be able to participate in this type of activity for five to ten minutes.

Activity: Spot the Difference

This visual attention activity is more interactive than the look-and-find activities listed above.

Intended Outcomes:

- Children will improve selective-attention skills.

- Children will improve visual-memory skills.
- Children will improve visual attention as they sustain their attention to the activity.

Materials:

- Clothing
- Hats
- Scarves
- Jewelry
- Glasses
- Handbag
- Backpack

What to Do:

1. Choose one child to be the person who will change their appearance. Invite this child to step behind a door or curtain or inside a closet or bathroom to put on some items.
2. When the child comes out, give the rest of the group thirty seconds to observe what the child is wearing. Encourage children to state out loud specific details that they notice about the child's appearance.
3. After the thirty seconds, the child hides while they change their appearance. To alter how they look, the child may add clothing, such as a hat, scarf, or sweater, or props, such as sunglasses, a purse, or backpack.
4. When their appearance has been altered, ask the child to present themselves to the group once again.
5. Invite the group to work together to identify how the child has altered their appearance.
6. Repeat this game with different children and props as long as time permits.

Listening Activities

Games such as Bingo require active-listening skills. These types of games encourage concentration and selective and sustained attention. Children must listen carefully to correctly hear what has been said while blocking out other sights and sounds happening around them. When children learn how to discern the differences in sounds, they improve both their concentration and memory skills.

Activity: What Did You Hear?

This game helps children learn how to focus and pay attention to a sound to identify it. Children listen intentionally to a sound being played and then guess what made the sound.

Intended Outcomes:

- Children will improve their memory as they recall the different sounds objects or animals make.
- Children will improve their concentration as they sustain their attention to guess the correct object based on the sound they hear.
- Children will improve their selective attention as they block out distracting sounds to focus on the sounds they hear while the game is played.
- Children will improve early literacy skills.

Materials:

- Audio of different sounds, such as a baby crying, cat meowing, car horn blowing, piano playing, and so on
- Kiddopedia has developed a variety of guess-the-sound challenges available for free on YouTube. Some of these include the sounds of household items, musical instruments, farm animal sounds, and vehicle sounds.

What to Do:

1. Before introducing this game to the class, decide how children will listen to different sounds. You may use a premade YouTube video or create your own sequence of different sounds.
2. Gather the class together and explain that they will be playing a game in which they listen to different sounds and guess what it is they hear. As an example, play a sound and ask the children what they think make that sound.
3. Once everyone understands how to play the game, remind them they will need to use their ears to listen for the sounds and their brains to remember what objects make that sound.
4. Start the audio, making sure there is enough time between sounds for children to think about and guess the object that makes that sound.
5. Continue playing for as long as time permits and/or as long as the children remain attentive to the activity.

Sorting Activities

Sorting is a developmentally appropriate activity for two- to six-year-olds to engage in to improve their understanding of same and different, to look at specifics, and to improve their cognitive skills. It also teaches sustained attention and focus skills. Sorting objects not only teaches important cognitive skills such as color or shape identification but also helps young children focus their attention on a specific attribute.

Activity: Savvy Sorter

For this activity, children will learn to sort by color, size, and/or shape. Choose a simple sorting activity for very young children, such as a two- or three-color sorting activity with two- and three-year-olds. Make sure the items to be sorted are the same and then choose two or three highly contrasting colors such as blue, red, and yellow.

Older children can also benefit from sorting activities. To make the activity more challenging for five- and six-year-olds, encourage them to sort by two or three characteristics at once. For example, in addition to sorting by color or shape, have them sort by color, shape, and/or size. Use objects such as buttons that vary in color, shape (circle, square, star, heart, and so on), and size. Demonstrate how to sort the objects by multiple characteristics, such as color and size, or color, size, and shape. This approach challenges older children and helps develop their sustained and selective attention skills.

Intended Outcomes:

- Children will improve their sorting skills.
- Children will work on attention to detail as they sort different colors, shapes, or other objects.
- Children will improve their sustained attention skills.

Materials:

- Muffin tin, small plastic containers, or baskets
- Items for sorting, such as pompoms, beads, buttons, and/or small plastic bears

What to Do:

1. Gather children together and talk with the group about what sorting means. Explain that sorting means grouping similar objects together based on one attribute, such as color or size. Reinforce that sorting means placing items in a group because they are alike in some way.
2. Show the children what objects they will be sorting, and explain which similarity they will be looking for: color, size, shape, and so on.
3. Demonstrate how to sort by placing similar objects together in a container or muffin tin.
4. Encourage the children to stick with the activity until all of the items have been sorted into groups.

Putting It All Together

A positive learning environment helps children feel confident and connected to their peers and the materials they interact with. Using metacognitive strategies to teach children how to think about the senses they need to focus and pay attention will support these skills. Finally, encouraging children to engage in visual attention and listening games targeted at teaching children attending skills will ensure that all children learn how to focus and pay attention to the best of their ability.

In chapter 7, the final chapter of this book, we explore how to apply the strategies discussed throughout the book to support attention and focus during specific parts of the day, including center time, circle time, and mealtimes.

Chapter 7
Supporting Attention and Focus throughout the Day

Attention and focus are skills that children learn and continue to improve as they get older. This makes early learning environments an excellent place to embed supports to help develop and nurture these skills. This chapter describes how using auditory and visual supports and creating consistency throughout the day will help young children remain alert and attentive. The remainder of this chapter discusses strategies to help children learn how to focus and sustain their attention during mealtimes, circle time, and center time.

Using Auditory Supports

Consider using auditory cues throughout the day to support sustained and selective attention skills. Auditory cues, such as songs, chimes, and chants, are useful sensory tools to help students manage their time and transition between activities. To be effective, teachers will need to teach and use these tools consistently. Once the children understand what each cue means, they will be better able to smoothly transition from one activity to the next. Common auditory supports include the following:

- Chant or song
- Gong or small drum
- Tambourine, triangle, or small xylophone

Chant or Song

Singing a simple chant or song can help children complete a common routine like cleaning up toys or handwashing. Songs and chants can also help young children more easily transition from one activity to another. Using a chant or song to help students complete common classroom routines is a fun and effective way to engage them while reinforcing structure and expectations. Here's an example of how Mr. Peters uses a bell to help his kindergarten students move smoothly from rest time to literacy.

> In a kindergarten classroom, transitions between activities can sometimes be challenging, especially for children who may have trouble shifting focus. A few of Mr. Peters's students struggle with this in the afternoon when they return to the classroom after lunch and recess. To help guide his students during this difficult part of the day, Mr. Peters uses a bell as auditory cue to signal to the class when it's time to move on to the next activity. It is rest and quiet choice time, so children are engaged in different activities—some are resting, while others are drawing or reading. Mr. Peters knows that it's almost time to transition to language arts, but he wants to ensure that the children have enough time to wrap up their current activities and prepare for the next task.
>
> Mr. Peters picks up his small bell, a familiar tool he always uses for transitions. He shakes it gently, producing a soft, calming sound. Then, he waits for a moment until the sound of the bell catches the children's attention. As the sound fades, Mr. Peters reminds the class what the bell means. He says, "That's our signal to start wrapping up. Can everyone hear the bell? It's time to start cleaning up and getting ready for circle time."
>
> Mr. Peters has used this bell all year so the students know that when they hear the bell, it's time to pause their current activity and prepare for the next one. But, since this is a challenging part of the day, he gives the class a quick

reminder: "Please finish up what you're doing and put your toys or books back where they belong. We'll be staring language arts in just a minute." Some students still need a little extra guidance, so Mr. Peters rings the bell again, reminding the students to focus and finish up. The bell not only serves as a gentle auditory cue but also reinforces a routine that the children have come to recognize. By using the bell, Mr. Peters creates a calm and consistent way for his students to transition smoothly from one activity to the next, ensuring that the classroom stays organized and that the children understand what is expected of them.

Musical Instruments

Use gongs or small drums, tambourines, triangles, or xylophones to signal to young children that it is time to begin or end an activity. You can also use a chime from a small xylophone or metal triangle to alert children that it is time to transition from one activity to another. Coupled with a chant or song, these sounds help children smoothly transition.

Using Visual Supports

Visual supports are useful tools to help children with time management while supporting attention and focus. They help children understand how long they have to wait for something to occur, how much longer an activity might last, and what activities will occur and in what order. Common visual supports include the following:

- Visual timers
- Visual schedules
- Sign-up systems

Visual Timers

A visual timer helps young children learn to understand time and how it passes. Instead of a clock face, a colored disk represents how much time there is for each activity. As time passes, the color disappears. When all of the color is gone, the time is up. When children need to wait for a short period of time, perhaps one, three, or five minutes, sand timers may be used. This type of visual support helps children understand how long they have until an activity ends and also helps them remain focused on the task at hand.

Visual Schedules

A visual schedule uses pictures and words to show the day's plan. Post a visual schedule in a spot in the classroom where children can easily reference it. This helps them know when it's time for free play, mealtime, and other parts of the day. A visual schedule also helps children learn how to independently manage their time, hunger, and patience.

Sign-Up Systems

Use a sign-up system for activities and centers to help children manage their turns so everyone gets a chance. One way children may sign up for a center activity might be to use a picture-based sign-in system.

- First, create a set of pictures or photographs that represent each center.
- Then, create a sign-in card for each child with their photo and name on it.
- Affix Velcro dots to the center photo and on the back of each child's card.
- When center time begins, each child places their card on the center activity they've chosen.

This allows all children, including those who are not writing yet, to sign in to the center they'd like to engage with. It also helps children see when a center is full or has room for them to join. The system makes it clear to both staff and students which centers are available and which children are in each area, which can be helpful for classroom management and supporting children's patience.

Creating Consistency throughout the Day

To create a consistent environment that supports young children's ability to focus and engage, consider implementing the following strategies throughout the day.

Follow a Daily Schedule

Develop and follow a daily class schedule that is similar each day. Talk about the daily schedule and post a visual to remind children of the order of the daily activities. When young children know what to expect, they are better able to sustain their attention on the activity they should be engaged in.

Teach and Support Common Routines

Classroom routines are activities and rules that establish clear expectations for children, which helps with classroom management and flow. When classroom routines are consistent, children are more independent, less distracted, and have fewer behaviors that challenge their learning, socializing, and safety.

In a kindergarten classroom, following rules and routines is essential for creating a safe and productive learning environment. Ms. Janie understands the importance of modeling these behaviors for her students, as young children learn best through observation. Here's an example of how she uses modeling to help her students follow the rules and routines of the classroom.

> Ms. Janie's class is full of eager kindergartners who are still learning how to navigate the structure of a school day. One of the classroom routines is the transition between activities, which can sometimes lead to distractions or confusion. Ms. Janie notices that some students struggle to follow the routine when it's time to clean up and move on to the next activity. A few students continue working even when she's given a cue that it's time to clean up. Some leave their

work at their desk and transition to the next activity without cleaning up their materials.

One morning, instead of simply giving directions that it is time to clean up, Ms. Janie decides to model the transition for her class. She announces, "Okay, class, it's time to clean up and get ready for math. Let's all work together." She starts by cleaning up her own area, placing her supplies in the designated basket and neatly stacking her books. She speaks clearly and calmly as she moves, saying, "I'm putting my pencils away in the cubby so they don't roll off the table."

As she continues, she encourages the students by saying, "I'm putting my papers in the recycling bin so we can keep our classroom clean. Can you find your papers and put them in the bin, too?" She moves around the room, offering gentle reminders and modeling how to pick up and put away supplies. As the students begin to follow her lead, Ms. Janie continues to reinforce the importance of following the routine with positive reinforcement. "I see Kiri is already putting her crayons away! Great job, Kiri!" she praises, motivating the other students to stay on task.

When the classroom is clean and everyone is ready for math, Ms. Janie models how to transition to the carpet. She says, "Now, it's time for us to go to the carpet for math. Let's walk quietly, and when we get there, we'll find a spot and sit down." She walks slowly and deliberately, setting the example for her students, who follow behind her.

By modeling the transition with calmness and clarity, Ms. Janie helps her students understand the importance of following the routine. She provides gentle reminders, offers praise for efforts, and reinforces the behaviors that contribute to a smooth, well-organized classroom. This structured approach helps the kindergartners develop a sense of responsibility and learn how to follow the rules and routines, making them feel secure and capable in their classroom environment. Common classroom routines could include teaching children:

- Raising your hand to ask a question
- Handwashing
- How to walk quietly through the hallway
- Transitioning from home to school
- Transitioning from school to home

Following established classroom routines provides structure and reduces the cognitive load, allowing children to easily understand expectations without having to think extensively about what their next steps should be. Once daily routines are familiar to children, they are more inclined to feel comfortable and confident in the classroom. They also have more attentional capacity to focus on learning and socializing.

Use visual and auditory supports to help young children remember these common routines. Posting visual cues, such as the daily routine or a visual highlighting the steps to complete handwashing, will help children remember and follow the steps independently.

Provide auditory supports or prompts such as a chant or song while the routine is happening to help children focus and attend to the activity. Use a bell or drum beat to let them know when an activity is ending or about to end, which will help them with time management and sustained attention.

Practicing common routines frequently helps make them consistent and easy. Young children are still learning the proper way to wash their hands, transition from home to school, and clean up their toys. These are skills that they are just acquiring, so they need time and practice to memorize how to complete each routine correctly. Once a child becomes familiar with a routine, their mental energy is free to focus more on learning and socializing.

Provide Frequent Breaks throughout the Day

As referenced in chapter 4, the amount of time a child can pay attention is limited. When they reach their limit, a child becomes unable to sustain their attention to the task at hand. One way to help children restore their attention span is to incorporate frequent breaks from learning and/or the classroom environment throughout the day.

- Limit the length of time children engage in learning activities, based on age.
- Take a nature break. Try to take breaks from the classroom environment to spend time outdoors at least once per day.
- Take learning or brain breaks during lengthier sedentary activities.
- Take learning breaks between organized classroom activities.

Supporting Attention and Focus during Specific Parts of the Day

Supporting children's attention and focus throughout the day helps them engage with learning and daily routines. Different parts of the day require different strategies to help children maintain their attention and focus.

Mealtimes

Mealtime is an excellent time to encourage children to socialize with their peers while working on self-help skills. This requires children to multitask or divide their attention, which is a difficult skill for children younger than six years of age (Ruff and Rothbart, 1996; Wray et al., 2017). When young children attempt to multitask during a snack or meal, they may have difficulty focusing on the food before them. Some children might struggle to finish eating in a timely manner. A variety of strategies can enhance mealtimes, making them both social and productive.

- Modeling
- Eating with the class
- Embedding time management
- Limiting distractions

During lunch time, model for young children how to stay attentive to the food and drinks before you. Talk about the food you are eating, maybe mentioning the color, taste, or types of food that are part of the meal. And model actually eating and drinking. Sit down at the table and eat with the class.

Embed time-management strategies into mealtime to help young children understand how long they have to eat their food. For example, give a five-minute warning and then a one-minute warning to alert children that mealtime is almost finished.

When children are distracted while they eat, they tend to eat less and feel hungry again more quickly later in the day. Children's attention is already divided between eating and socializing, so limiting unnecessary visual and auditory distractions is an important step to helping them focus on eating their food in the allotted time. For those children who eat their meals and snacks in the classroom, noise volume, overhead lighting, and people moving around the classroom can make it hard to focus on eating. Most kindergarten and first-grade students eat in the school cafeteria. In the lunchroom, various visual and auditory distractions can affect students' ability to focus on eating. Children moving between tables or getting up to use the restroom and students' conversations can be overstimulating and distracting to some children. Seeing other students engage in social interactions or misbehaving can further distract children from eating. Harsh lighting can also cause visual discomfort, making it harder for students to stay focused on their meal. However, there are measures that can help diminish these distractions both within the classroom or in the cafeteria.

- Create quieter zones for students who need less stimulation. These areas could be positioned away from high-traffic zones, such as entrances, or loud group activities.
- Avoid seating children near distractions, such as the lunch line, front door, or groups of students who tend to be loud.
- Consider seating students in small groups to minimize constant visual stimuli and help them focus on their meal.

- Keep the walls of the classroom and lunchroom environment simple. Avoid overly bright, busy, or cluttered bulletin boards and posters that might distract children from eating.
- Use natural light or dim the overhead lights, if possible, to reduce harsh glare and make the space more comfortable.
- Encourage students to stay seated during lunch to reduce distractions caused by people walking around. Allow movement for specific reasons, such as getting additional napkins or using the restroom.

Modeling is another effective strategy to improve children's focus and attention during mealtimes. Eating lunch with students and modeling desired behaviors, such as attention and focus, can be an effective strategy to help children stay engaged and avoid distractions. Here's an example of how Ms. Sydney uses modeling to help her first-grade students focus on eating their lunch in the cafeteria.

> Ms. Sydney's class is one of five first-grade classrooms. All of first grade eats lunch at the same time, which makes the cafeteria a noisy and lively place. She has noticed that some students eat very little during the allotted lunchtime and often come to her later in the day asking for a snack because they're still hungry. One afternoon, instead of sitting with the other first-grade teachers, Ms. Sydney decides to sit with her class. She asks if it's okay to join them, sets down her tray, and begins eating. She remains calm and focused on her meal, avoiding distractions like looking around the room or engaging in non-lunch topics. She encourages her students to eat their food and models how to eat slowly, take small bites, and chew properly. When Sophie becomes distracted by the noisy table next to them, Ms. Sydney comments, "Wow, it's loud in here! I'm going to focus on eating so I can finish my meal and enjoy it. That way I won't be hungry later." As the students' focus begins to wane, Ms. Sydney engages them by asking simple, relevant questions. "Sophie, what's your favorite part of your lunch today?" She waits for Sophie to answer, taking intentional bites of her food and listening carefully. Joey, sitting next to

> Sophie, is eating a sandwich. Ms. Sydney asks, "Can you tell me what's inside your sandwich?" She continues asking her students questions about their meals while modeling good eating habits. This helps the children stay focused on their food and encourages social interaction. Ms. Sydney shows her class that eating can be both enjoyable and focused. By actively eating and demonstrating good habits, she encourages her students to imitate these behaviors. This helps the children learn by example and reinforces the focus on eating. As lunchtime comes to an end, Ms. Sydney models how to clean up. She begins to clean her area and says, "We're almost done. Let's start by cleaning up our wrappers and putting away our lunches."

By modeling calm, focused eating behavior, offering gentle redirection when necessary, and providing positive reinforcement, Ms. Sydney helps her students stay engaged during lunch, develop healthy eating habits, and create an enjoyable, social lunchtime experience.

Circle Time

During whole-group time, children need strong attention and focus skills as they pay attention to the person speaking, wait their turn, and share and engage in a large group. This can be a challenging time of the day for young children to sit and sustain their attention on their own. To help them, keep activities short and interactive. This doesn't mean that the length of circle time needs to be short. If activities that are part of the circle-time experience last for an age-appropriate amount of time, young children should be able to sit and attend for up to twenty minutes. When circle time consists of a combination of movement breaks and engaging learning content, most young children can attend for fifteen to twenty minutes with no difficulty. Consider the following example describing how Ms. Chavis uses movement, tactile, visual, and auditory supports to help the children in her class focus and sustain their attention during circle time.

> When center time ends, preschool teacher Ms. Chavis calls the children to circle time by banging a small drum. As

they transition to the space, Ms. Chavis welcomes them to the carpet and reminds them to find a spot and sit down. She lets them know that they will be talking and learning about their senses. She spends a few minutes describing the five senses and then allows the children to share or ask questions. While she talks, she passes around a plastic ear, a toy eyeball, and a rubber brain for children to interact with. Next, she taps the small gong that sits on her desk and asks the students to see how long they can hear the sound. She asks them which sense they use to listen with, and the child who has the toy ear holds it up. Next, Ms. Chavis reads a short book about the senses. She encourages the children to describe times they've used their senses to smell, touch, taste, and see things. Finally, she taps the gong again, encouraging the children to close their eyes to see how long they can hear the sound. Before transitioning away from circle time, Ms. Chavis gives instructions for the seated activity the students will work on next.

In this example, Ms. Chavis uses auditory, visual, and tactile supports to help her students actively participate in each of the circle time activities.

Center Time

To support sustained attention, focus, and concentration during centers, consider matching the children's capacity for attention and focus with the time each center activity lasts. For example, if center time lasts for a total of thirty minutes, then a classroom made of up mostly of three-year-olds could engage in a total of four center activities. Students can spend approximately seven minutes at each center before switching to the next activity.

In contrast, a prekindergarten class of four- and five-year-olds have the attentional capacity to engage in two to three center activities lasting ten to thirteen minutes long in that same thirty-minute block of time. Or, for this group of older children, center time may last forty-five minutes instead of thirty, which would allow for four different center activities. Center time typically lasts for a designated block of time, but it is often flexible, allowing children to move between centers and revisit activities as they choose. However, the teacher may set guidelines for how long children can stay at each center and when it's time to transition to a new activity.

During center time, children choose activities and explore in small groups at stations located around the classroom. These activities are usually child-led, meaning students may interact with and explore the activity the way they want. Because centers are child-led, children are better able to sustain their attention to the activity at hand. However, all children benefit from visual and auditory supports to bolster their sustained and selective attention. These supports might include visual times, chants, or chimes to facilitate transitions; visual schedules; and sensory supports.

Embed visual supports throughout center time to help children with sustained and selective attention. Common visual supports include a visual schedule highlighting available center activities, a sign-up system to help children understand which centers have available space and which ones are full, and photographs taped to storage to help children remember where to locate desired items and where to place them when it is time to clean up. Visual schedules made up of pictures and labels that outline the sequence of activities during center time help children know what will come next. This will help children independently manage expectations and time more effectively.

Embed time-management strategies into center time to support sustained attention to the task at hand while also helping young children understand how long they have to wait until the next center activity starts. Common time-management strategies include the following:

- Use a visual timer to show how much time exists for each activity.
- Use sand timers to help individual children understand how much time they need to wait to transition to the next activity.
- Provide a five-minute warning and a one-minute warning to cue children that the center activity will end soon.

Supporting center time with sensory inputs is an excellent way to increase engagement. Multisensory activities encourage sustained attention and skill acquisition because children have multiple ways to connect with materials and topics. The more interested and engaged children are in an activity, the less likely they will become bored or frustrated when they make a mistake.

Here's an example of how Ms. Curry uses sensory inputs to help her students stay focused and sustain their attention during center time.

> Ms. Curry has been a prekindergarten teacher for over a decade, and during this time, she's noticed a shift in her students' attention spans, especially during center time. In the past, her students loved the drawing and building centers. Recently, however, she's observed that more children are wandering between centers, requiring support to refocus, or having difficulty engaging in activities independently. In an effort to improve sustained attention and encourage independence, Ms. Curry decides to add sensory inputs to each of the center activities. At the drawing station, in addition to white paper, she introduces colorful paper, sandpaper, felt, and wrapping paper. She also adds scented markers and shaped crayons (crayons in fun shapes such as animals, stars, and eggs). These additions provide a mix of olfactory, visual, and tactile stimulation, which may help students stay more focused on their drawings for longer. To enhance the building center, Ms. Curry incorporates magnets, colorful blocks, and textured materials like small rubber mats, sandpaper, and felt. She also adds visuals of buildings, bridges, and cityscapes to inspire students and help them imagine what they could create. After introducing these new sensory elements, Ms. Curry encourages the children to explore and get creative. The response is immediate. The class is excited and engaged, eager to explore the new sensory inputs. By integrating these sensory elements into center time, Ms. Curry has successfully helped her students remain engaged and attentive.

Putting It All Together

Limiting the time children spend seated during activities to match the average age of the class helps them maintain attention on what they are doing. Regular breaks between activities and during longer seated activities will also help restore children's ability to focus throughout the day. Teach, practice, and reinforce common routines until children become familiar with them. When children have routines memorized, they no longer need to think about each step, freeing up mental energy so that they have more capacity to focus and attend to organized learning activities.

Implementing these strategies throughout the day ensures that children can stayed focused and attentive. Providing children with visual, auditory, time-management, and sensory supports will help them stay focused, engaged, and excited about learning!

References and Recommended Readings

Abbasi, Ali M., et al. 2019. "The Impact of Indoor Air Temperature on the Executive Functions of Human Brain and the Physiological Responses of Body." *Health Promotion Perspectives* 9(1): 55–64. https://doi.org/10.15171/hpp.2019.07

Ayres, A. Jean. 1972. *Sensory Integration and Learning Disorders.* Western Psychological Services.

Benedict, Elizabeth A., Robert H. Horner, and Jane K. Squires. 2007. "Assessment and Implementation of Positive Behavior Support in Preschools." *Topics in Early Childhood Special Education* 27(3): 174–192.

Berman, Marc G., John Jonides, and Stephen Kaplan. 2008. "The Cognitive Benefits of Interacting with Nature." *Psychological Science* 19(12): 1207–1212.

Brandes-Aitken, Annie, et al. 2019. "Sustained Attention in Infancy: A Foundation for the Development of Multiple Aspects of Self-Regulation for Children in Poverty." *Journal of Experimental Child Psychology* 184: 192–209.

Boyce, Peter, et al. 2006. "Lighting Quality and Office Work: Two Field Simulation Experiments." *Lighting Research and Technology* 38(3): 191–233.

Bundy, Anita C., Shelly J. Lane, and Elizabeth A. Murray. 2002. *Sensory Integration: Theory and Practice.* 2nd edition. F. A. Davis.

Carroll, Paul. 2022. "Effectiveness of Positive Discipline Parenting Program on Parenting Style and Child Adaptive Behavior." *Child Psychiatry and Human Development* 53(6): 1349–1358.

Cohen, Ronald. 1993. *The Neuropsychology of Attention.* Springer.

Cohen, Ronald, Ilan Lohr, Robert Paul, and Robert Boland, R. 2001. "Impairments of Attention and Effort among Patients with Major Affective Disorders." *Journal of Neuropsychiatry and Clinical Neurosciences* 13(3): 385–395.

Dee, Thomas S., and Emily K. Penner. 2017. "The Causal Effects of Cultural Relevance: Evidence from an Ethnic Studies Curriculum." *American Educational Research Journal* 54(1): 127–166.

Derryberry, Douglas, and Mary K. Rothbart. 1997. "Reactive and Effortful Processes in the Organization of Temperament." *Development and Psychopathology* 9(4): 633–652.

Fischer, Susanne, et al. 2024. "Emerging Effects of Temperature on Human Cognition, Affect, and Behaviour." *Biological Psychology* 189: 108791. https://doi.org/10.1016/j.biopsycho.2024.108791

Fortenbaugh, Francesca C., Joseph DeGutis, and Michael Esterman. 2017. "Recent Theoretical, Neural, and Clinical Advances in Sustained Attention Research." *Annals of the New York Academy of Sciences* 1396(1): 70–91.

Gallen, Courtney L., et al. 2023. "Contribution of Sustained Attention Abilities to Real-World Academic Skills in Children." *Scientific Reports* 13(1): 2673.

Gomes, Hilary, et al. 2000. "The Development of Auditory Attention in Children." *Frontiers in Bioscience* 5(3): D108–D120.

Gunn, AnnMarie A., et al. 2020. "Revisiting Culturally Responsive Teaching Practices for Early Childhood Preservice Teachers." *Journal of Early Childhood Teacher Education* 42(3): 265–280.

Hawkins, J. David, et al. 2001. "Long-Term Effects of the Seattle Social Development Intervention on School Bonding Trajectories." *Applied Developmental Science* 5(4): 225–236.

Jones, Pete R., David R. Moore, and Sygal Amitay. 2015. "Development of Auditory Selective Attention: Why Children Struggle to Hear in Noisy Environments." *Developmental Psychology* 51(3): 353–369.

Haverinen-Shaughnessy, Ulla, and Richard J. Shaughnessy. 2015. "Effects of Classroom Ventilation Rate and Temperature on Students' Test Scores." *PLoS ONE* 10(8): e0136165. https://doi.org/10.1371/journal.pone.0136165

Kaplan, Rachel, and Stephen Kaplan. 1989. *The Experience of Nature: A Psychological Perspective*. Cambridge University Press.

Kaplan, Stephen. 1995. "The Restorative Benefits of Nature: Toward an Integrative Framework." *Journal of Environmental Psychology* 15(3): 169–182.

Kaplan, Stephen, and Marc G. Berman. 2010. "Directed Attention as a Common Resource for Executive Functioning and Self-Regulation." *Perspectives on Psychological Science* 5(1): 43–57.

Ko, Li-Wei, et al. 2017. "Sustained Attention in Real Classroom Settings: An EEG Study." *Frontiers in Human Neuroscience* 11: 388. https://doi.org/10.3389/fnhum.2017.00388

Krauzlis, Richard J., Lupeng Wang, Gongchen Yu, and Leor N. Katz. 2023. "What Is Attention?" *Wiley Interdisciplinary Reviews (WIREs) Cognitive Science* 14(1): e1570. https://doi.org/10.1002/wcs.1570

Lai, Yi-Jung, and Kang-Ming Chang. 2020. "Improvement of Attention in Elementary School Students through Fixation Focus Training Activity." *International Journal of Environmental Research and Public Health* 17(13): 4780. https://doi.org/10.3390/ijerph17134780

Lee, Hoo Young, Sung Eun Hyun, and Byung-Mo Oh. 2022. "Rehabilitation for Impaired Attention in the Acute and Post-Acute Phase After Traumatic Brain Injury: A Narrative Review." *Korean Journal of Neurotrauma* 19(1): 20–31.

Lee, Phyllis, and Karen L. Bierman. 2015. "Classroom and Teacher Support in Kindergarten: Associations with the Behavioral and Academic Adjustment of Low-Income Students." *Merrill Palmer Quarterly* 61(3): 383–411.

Lev-Ari, Tidhar, Hadar Beeri, and Yoram Gutfreund. 2022. "The Ecological View of Selective Attention." *Frontiers in Integrative Neuroscience* 16: 856207. https://doi.org/10.3389/fnint.2022.856207

Lin, Hung-Yu. 2022. "The Effects of White Noise on Attentional Performance and On-Task Behaviors in Preschoolers with ADHD." *International Journal of Environmental Research and Public Health* 19(22): 15391. https://doi.org/10.3390/ijerph192215391

Lodge, Jason M., and William J. Harrison. 2019. "The Role of Attention in Learning in the Digital Age." *Yale Journal of Biology and Medicine* 92(1): 21–28.

Mason, Lucia, Angelica Ronconi, Sara Scrimin, and Francesca Pazzaglia. 2022. "Short-Term Exposure to Nature and Benefits for Students' Cognitive Performance: A Review." *Educational Psychology Review* 34: 609–647.

Mason, Lucia, et al. 2022. "Children's Attentional Processes in Outdoor and Indoor Environments: The Role of Physiological Self-Regulation." *International Journal of Environmental Research and Public Health* 19(20): 13141. https://doi.org/10.3390/ijerph192013141

May-Benson, Teresa A., and Jane A. Koomar. 2010. "Systematic Review of the Research Evidence Examining the Effectiveness of Interventions Using a Sensory Integrative Approach for Children." *American Journal of Occupational Therapy* 64(3): 403–414.

McClelland, Megan M., et al. 2007. "Links between Behavioral Regulation and Preschoolers' Literacy, Vocabulary, and Math Skills." *Developmental Psychology* 43(4): 947–959.

McClelland, Megan M., Claire E. Cameron, Shannon B. Wanless, and Amy Murray. 2007. "Executive Function, Behavioral Self-Regulation, and Social-Emotional Competence: Links to School Readiness." In *Contemporary Perspectives on Social Learning in Early Childhood Education.* Information Age Publishing.

McClelland, Megan M., et al. 2013. "Relations between Preschool Attention Span-Persistence and Age 25 Educational Outcomes." *Early Childhood Research Quarterly* 28(2): 314–324.

McCormick, Rachel. 2017. "Does Access to Green Space Impact the Mental Well-Being of Children: A Systematic Review." *Journal of Pediatric Nursing* 37: 3–7. https://doi.org/10.1016/j.pedn.2017.08.027

Ohly, Heather, et al. 2016. "Attention Restoration Theory: A Systematic Review of the Attention Restoration Potential of Exposure to Natural Environments." *Journal of Toxicology and Environmental Health, Part B* 19(7): 305–343.

Oken, Barry S., M. C. Salinsky, and Siegward M. Elsas. 2006. "Vigilance, Alertness, or Sustained Attention: Physiological Basis and Measurement." *Clinical Neurophysiology* 117(9): 1885–1901.

Plebanek, Daniel J., and Vladimir M. Sloutsky. 2017. "Costs of Selective Attention: When Children Notice What Adults Miss." *Psychological Science* 28(6): 723–732.

Posner, Michael I., Mary K. Rothbart, Brad E. Sheese, and Pascale Voelker. 2014. "Developing Attention: Behavioral and Brain Mechanisms." *Advances in Neuroscience* 2014(1): 405094. https://doi.org/10.1155/2014/405094

Razza, Rachel A., Anne Martin, and Jeanne Brooks-Gunn. 2010. "Associations among Family Environment, Sustained Attention, and School Readiness for Low-Income Children." *Developmental Psychology* 46(6): 1528–1542.

Ruff, Holly A., and Mary K. Rothbart. 1996. *Attention in Early Development: Themes and Variations.* Oxford University Press.

Schertz, Kathryn E., et al. 2022. "Environmental Influences on Affect and Cognition: A Study of Natural and Commercial Semi-Public Spaces." *Journal of Environmental Psychology* 83: 1–13.

Shield, Bridget M., and Julie E. Dockrell. 2008. "The Effects of Environmental and Classroom Noise on the Attention and Task Performance of Primary School Children." *Journal of the Acoustical Society of America* 123(1): 133–144.

Slattery, Eadaoin, Patrick Ryan, Donal G. Fortune, and Laura P. McAvinue. 2022. "Unique and Overlapping Contributions of Sustained Attention and Working Memory to Parent and Teacher Ratings of Inattentive Behavior." *Child Neuropsychology* 28(6): 791–813.

Smolders, Karin C. H. J., and Yvonne A. W. de Kort. 2014. "Bright Light and Mental Fatigue: Effects on Alertness, Vitality, Performance, and Physiological Arousal." *Journal of Environmental Psychology* 39: 77–91.

Sohlberg, McKay M., and Catherine A. Mateer. 1987. "Effectiveness of an Attention-Training Program." *Journal of Clinical and Experimental Neuropsychology* 9(2): 117–130.

Stansfield, Stephen, and Charlotte Clark. 2015. "Health Effects of Noise Exposure in Children." *Current Environmental Health Reports* 2(2): 171–178.

Towe-Goodman, Nissa, et al. 2024. "Green Space and Internalizing or Externalizing Symptoms Among Children." *JAMA Network Open* 7(4): e245742. https://doi.org/10.1001/jamanetworkopen.2024.5742

van Oordt, Menno, Kim Ouwehand, and Fred Paas. 2022. "Restorative Effects of Observing Natural and Urban Scenery after Working Memory Depletion." *International Journal of Environmental Research and Public Health.* 20(1): 188. https://doi.org/10.3390/ijerph20010188

Vanaken, Gert-Jan, and Marina Danckaerts. 2018. "Impact of Green Space Exposure on Children's and Adolescents' Mental Health: A Systematic Review." *International Journal of Environmental Research and Public Health* 15(12): 2668. https://doi.org/10.3390/ijerph15122668

Watzl, Sebastian. 2023. "What Attention Is. The Priority Structure Account." *Wiley Interdisciplinary Reviews (WIREs) Cognitive Science* 14(1): e1632. https://doi.org/10.1002/wcs.1632

Wilkins, Natalie J., Jorge M. V. Verlenden, Leigh E. Szucs, and Michelle M. Johns. 2023. "Classroom Management and Facilitation Approaches That Promote School Connectedness." *Journal of School Health* 93(7): 582–593.

Williford, Amanda P., et al. 2013. "Understanding How Children's Engagement and Teachers' Interactions Combine to Predict School Readiness." *Journal of Applied Developmental Psychology* 34(6): 299–309.

Wray, Amanda H., et al. 2017. "Development of Selective Attention in Preschool-Age Children from Lower Socioeconomic Status Backgrounds." *Developmental Cognitive Neuroscience* 26: 101–111.

Index

A

active listening, 41, 42, 52, 97.
    See also listening activities
    activating the senses, 97–98
    can we do it a different way?, 49–50
    classroom red light, green light, 56–57
    learning with sensory bins, 83–84
    savvy sorter, 102–103
    spot the difference, 99–100
    what am I forgetting?, 52–53
    what did you hear?, 101–102
    what else can it be?, 50–51
    what's missing?, 54–55

arousal level
    about, 76–77
    auditory inputs and, 88–90
    movement inputs and, 90–92
    tactile games, activities, and inputs and, 77–84
    visual inputs and, 84–88

attention
    See also attention span; environmental considerations to support attention and focus
    about, v, 1–2
    adults and, v–vi, vi–vii
    auditory inputs and, 88–90
    cognitive skills and, vi
    components of, 2–10
    early learning classrooms and, 12–13
    educational games and activities that teach attention, 99–103
    example difficulty with, vii–viii
    executive function, attention, and focus, 39–40
    movement inputs and, 90–92
    natural environment and its restorative effect on, 69–72
    necessity of attention skills, 11–12
    rewarding focus and, 96
    self-regulation and, 17
    tactile games, activities, and inputs and, 77–84
    technology and, 10
    visual inputs and, 84–88
    what it is and why it matters, 1–13

attention restoration theory (ART), 72

attention span
    See also attention about, 2–4
    by age, 3, 95
    connection between attention span and executive function. *See* executive function
    self-regulation and, 15

attentional flexibility
    See also executive function
    about, ix, 35, 36
    activities to support, 48–51
    filtering and, 37
    flexible thinking and, 36
    modeling and, 44
    sustained attention and, 39
    task switching and, 37

auditory distractions
    See also distractions decreasing

auditory distractions, 89–90
mealtimes and, 113
physical environment and, 64
sustained attention and, 4–5

auditory inputs and supports
See also sensory inputs about, 31
center time and, 117
in circle time example, 115–116
filtering and, 37
as a sensory tool, 76
supporting attention and focus during specific parts of the day, 105–107
supporting attention, focus, and arousal, 88–90
teaching and supporting common routines, 111

auditory selective attention, 7
See also attention; selective attention

B

balance activities, 55, 90, 91
See also movement behavior
affects of self-regulation on, 17–19
social environments and, 65

breaks
nature breaks, 72
providing throughout the day, 111–112

C

calming visual inputs, 85–86
See also visual inputs and supports center time, supporting attention and focus during, 116–118
See also learning centers; supporting attention and focus throughout the day

chants or songs, 106–107
See also auditory inputs and supports

chunking, 38

circle time, supporting attention and focus during, 115–116
See also supporting attention and focus throughout the day

classroom management
classroom routines and, 109
positive supports and, 96
sign-up systems and, 108
social environment and, 65
visual inputs and, 84, 85, 86

classroom strategies to support executive function
See also executive function
about, 40
metacognition, 41–43
modeling, 44–46
role-play, 46–47
time management, 47–48

closed-ended activities, 27
See also open-ended play

components of attention
See also attention
about, 2
attention span, 2–4
divided attention, 8–10

selective attention, 5–8
sustained attention, 4–5

connection between attention span and executive function. *See* executive function

coregulation, practicing, 32–34
See also self-regulation

cueing
auditory supports and, 105–107
metacognition and, 41, 42, 43
mindfulness cues, 43
noise levels and, 31
time-management skills and, 48

cultural environment, 66–68
See also environmental considerations to support attention and focus

D

demonstrations, 20
See also modeling

distractions
decreasing auditory distractions, 89–90
mealtimes and, 113–114
organization and, 86, 87
physical environment and, 63–64
self-regulation and, 10
sustained attention and, 4–5

divided attention, 8–10, 40
See also attention

dynamic seating, 55

E

educational games and activities to teach and encourage focus and concentration
about, 95–96
attention, games and activities that teach, 99–103
metacognition, 97–98
positive supports, 96–97
putting it all together, 104

emotional regulation
See also self-regulation
coregulation and, 32–34
identifying and understanding feelings, 23–26
inhibitory control and, 36
modeling and, 19–22
open-ended play and, 26–28
self-regulation and, 18–19
sensory inputs and, 28–32

environmental considerations to support attention and focus
See also learning environments
about, 59–60
natural environment and, 69–72
physical environment and, 60–64
putting it all together, 73
social-emotional and cultural environments, 64–68

executive function
about, ix, 35–36
attention and, vi
attentional flexibility, 36–37
attentional flexibility, activities to

support, 48–51

classroom strategies to support, 40–48

executive function, attention, and focus, 39–40

inhibitory control, 39

inhibitory control, activities to support, 55–57

putting it all together, 58

working memory, 37–38

working memory, activities to support, 52–55

F

families and the cultural environment, 67

feelings, identifying and understanding, 23–26

fidget toys, 78–79

filtering, 37

See also attentional flexibility

fine-motor skills, 80

flexible thinking, 36, 40, 44

See also attentional flexibility

focus

See also educational games and activities to teach and encourage focus and concentration; environmental considerations to support attention and focus

auditory inputs and, 88–90

executive function, attention, and, 39–40

metacognition and, 43

movement inputs and, 90–92

natural environment and its restorative effect on, 69–72

rewarding, 96

self-regulation and, 15, 17

tactile games, activities, and inputs and, 77–84

technology and, 10

visual inputs and, 84–88

G

games and activities to teach and encourage focus and concentration

See educational games and activities to teach and encourage focus and attention

green spaces, 69, 70, 72

gross-motor skills, 32, 80

I

impulse control

metacognition and, 43

modeling, 45

self-regulation and, 16

inhibitory control

See also executive function

about, ix, 36, 39

activities to support, 55–57

attention and, vi

cueing and, 43

sustained and selective attention and, 40

instant gratification, 10, 16

introduction
- attention, v–viii
- how this book is organized, viii–x

L

learning centers
- center time, supporting attention and focus during, 116–118
- physical environment and, 62, 63
- sign-up systems and, 108

learning environments
- *See also* environmental considerations to support attention and focus
- creating supportive learning environments, 96–97
- lighting and, 61, 113, 114
- noise levels, 31, 89
- room arrangement and, 61–63
- room temperature and, 60–61
- sensory inputs and, 28–29
- visual distractions and, 30

lighting and the learning environment, 61, 113, 114

listening
- active listening, 41, 42, 52, 97
- activity: activating the senses, 97–98
- activity: what did you hear?, 101–102
- auditory distractions and, 64

M

manipulatives, 75, 79–80

mealtimes
- divided attention and, 9
- supporting attention and focus during, 112–115

messy inputs
- *See also* tactile inputs
- about, 29–30

messy tactile activities, 81–83

metacognition
- executive function and, 40, 41–43
- games and activities to teach and encourage focus and concentration and, 97–98

mindfulness cues, 43
- *See also* cueing

modeling
- active listening and, 42
- executive function and, 40, 44–46
- mealtimes and, 112, 114–115
- noise levels and, 31, 64
- practicing coregulation, 32–34
- self-regulation and, 19–22
- teaching and supporting common routines, 109–110

movement
- about movement inputs, 29, 32
- activities to support inhibitory control, 55–56
- in circle time example, 115–116
- incorporating movement inputs throughout the day, 91–92

incorporating movement into learning activities, 92
nature breaks and, 72
as a sensory tool, 76
supporting attention, focus, and arousal level, 90–92

multitasking, 9, 11, 39, 40, 112
See also divided attention

music and musical instruments, 31, 64, 88, 106–107
See also auditory input and supports

N

nature and the natural environment, 69–72, 112. See also environmental considerations to support attention and focus

noise levels, 31, 64, 89

O

obstacle courses, 91

open-ended play
emotional regulation and, 19
self-regulation and participating in, 26–28
sensory bins and, 83
tactile sensory play and, 80–81

organization/visual organization, 86–88

overstimulation, 10

P

patience
praising patience, 43
time management and, 47

physical learning environment, considerations for, 60–64
See also environmental considerations to support attention and focus; learning environments

play
See open-ended play

positive supports, 96–97

praise
positive supports, 96
praising patience, 43

R

rewarding focus and attention, 96

role-play.
See also modeling
executive function and, 40, 46–47
self-regulation and, 19, 20–22

room arrangements, 61–63
See also learning environments

room temperature, 60–61
See also learning environments

rules and routines
chants or songs and, 106
modeling rule following, 45–46
social environment and, 65, 66
teaching and supporting

common routines, 109–111
time-management skills and, 48
visual aids and, 86

S

savvy sorter activity, 102–103

schedules
breaks, providing throughout the day, 111–112
center time and, 117
creating consistency throughout the day, 109
visual schedules, use of, 30, 48, 107, 108, 117

seated activities, 92

selective attention
See also attention
about, 5–8
center time and, 117
inhibitory control and, 40

self-awareness, 25, 41, 43

self-control, ix, 40, 47, 48, 55

self-regulation
about, viii, 15–17
affect of on children's behaviors, 17–19
attention and, vi
coregulation, practicing, 32–34
identifying and understanding feelings, 23–26
importance of, 34
and its effects on attention and focus, 15–34
modeling, 19–22
participating in open-ended play, 26–28
sensory inputs, using, 28–32

self-talk, 41, 43

sensory bins, 82, 83–84

sensory inputs
about as a sensory tool, 75–76
arousal level and, 76–77
auditory inputs and supports, 31, 88–90, 105–107
center time and, 117
movement inputs and supports, 32, 90–92
putting it all together, 93
tactile games, activities, and inputs to support attention, focus, and arousal levels, 77–84
tactile or messy inputs, 29–30
using, 28–29
visual inputs and supports, 30, 84–88, 107–108

sensory inputs, games, and strategies to support attention and focus
See sensory inputs

sign-up systems, 108

Simon Says, 91

social environment, 65–66
See also environmental considerations to support attention and focus

sorting activities, 102–103

supporting attention and focus
throughout the day
about, 105
auditory supports and, 105–107
creating consistency throughout
the day, 109–112
putting it all together, 119
supporting attention and focus
during specific parts of the day,
112–118
visual supports and, 107–108

supportive learning environments,
creating, 96–97
See also learning environments

sustained attention
See also attention
about, 4–5
attentional flexibility and, 39
center time and, 117
executive functioning and, 39
inhibitory control and, 40
self-regulation and, 17, 18
technology and, 10
time management and, 47

T

tactile inputs.
See also sensory inputs
about, 29–30
activity: learning with sensory bins,
83–84
fidget toys and, 78–79
in circle time example, 115–116
manipulatives and, 79–80
messy tactile activities, 81–83

as a sensory tool, 75–76
tactile games, activities, and
inputs to support attention, focus,
and arousal levels, 77–84
tactile sensory play, 80–81
using sensory inputs, 28–29

task switching, 37, 44

technology and attention, 10

temperature/room temperature and
the learning environment, 60–61

time management
center time and, 117
classroom strategies to support
executive function, 40, 47–48
mealtimes and, 112, 113
visual inputs and, 30, 107

timers, 48, 85, 107–108, 117

transitions
center time and, 117
cues for, 48
incorporating movement input
throughout the day, 91
teaching and supporting
common routines, 110–111
time management and, 47, 48

V

visual aids, 86

visual distractions
See also distractions
mealtimes and, 113–114
organization and, 86, 87
physical learning environment

and, 63–64
sustained attention and, 4–5
visual inputs and supports, 30

visual inputs and supports
See also sensory inputs
about, 30
calming visual inputs, 85–86
center time and, 117
in circle time example, 115–116
filtering and, 37
as a sensory tool, 76
sign-up systems, 108
supporting attention and focus throughout the day, 107–108
supporting attention, focus, and arousal level, 84–88
teaching and supporting common routines, 111
visual activities, 99–100

visual organization, 86–88

visual schedules, use of, 30, 48, 107, 108, 117

visual selective attention, 7
See also attention; selective attention

visual timers, 107–108, 117

visuals and auditory input, 31

W

white noise, 31, 64, 89

working memory
See also executive function
about, ix, 35, 37–38

activities to support, 52–55
attention and, vi
cueing and, 42
divided attention and, 40
role-play and, 47